MEALS AND RECIPES
FROM ANCIENT GREECE

EUGENIA SALZA PRINA RICOTTI

Translated by Ruth Anne Lotero

MEALS AND RECIPES

FROM ANCIENT GREECE

J. PAUL GETTY MUSEUM, LOS ANGELES

Dedicated to the memory of my mother,
Luisa Cumbo Borgia,
and to the future of my nieces Giovanna and Luisa Salza
and my nephew, Filippo Salza

Italian edition © 2005 L'Erma di Bretschneider, Rome

English edition © 2007 J. Paul Getty Trust

Published by the J. Paul Getty Museum, Los Angeles
Getty Publications
1200 Getty Center Drive, Suite 500
Los Angeles, California 90049-1682
www.getty.edu

Mark Greenberg, *Editor in Chief*

Ann Lucke, *Managing Editor*
Robin H. Ray, *Editor*
Elizabeth Zozom and Pamela Heath, *Production Coordinators*
Markus Brilling, *Designer*

Drawings courtesy of the Research Library, The Getty Research Institute, Los Angeles

Library of Congress Cataloging-in-Publication Data

Salza Prina Ricotti, Eugenia.
  [L'arte del convito nella grecia antica. English]
  Meals and recipes from ancient Greece / Eugenia Salza Prina Ricotti; translated by Ruth Anne Lucero.
     p. cm.
  Includes bibliographic references and index.
  ISBN 978-0-89236-876-1 (hardcover)
  1. Cookery, Greek—History. 2. Food habits—Greece—History. I. Title.
  TX723.5.G8S3386 2007
  641.5'9495—dc22
                          2006024550

Typesetting by Diane Franco
Printed by Tien Wah Press, Singapore

CONTENTS

INTRODUCTION

From the age of Achilles to Alexander the Great: over a thousand years, and such a great span of history. And not just the courtly history of battles, plagues, kings, tyrants, and great orators, but also the plodding, daily history of common people trying to make the most out of life.

We can look back on ancient Greek life through its epic and wide-ranging literature, in which all subjects, including daily life, are explored. In this literature we find a wealth of information about ancient Greek meals, from those hosted by the Mycenaean kings to the fantastic banquets of the last sovereigns of the Hellenistic era. There are thousands of passages dealing with food and dining, everything from etiquette to menu planning. We are fortunate indeed that almost all the authors of the Hellenistic age—geographers, storytellers, chroniclers of history, poets, or, best of all, comic writers—wrote about food, banquets, and wine. (Intriguingly, almost all of these writers included voluntary purging as a topic.) Other scholars compiled books whose sole theme was the kitchen and its ingredients. We have evidence of well over twenty works specializing in cuisine of which, unfortunately, only a handful have survived.

The most important and complete of the surviving texts is the work of a Greek scholar, Athenaeus. Leaving behind his native Naucratis in Egypt, Athenaeus moved to Rome in the second century B.C. to become the librarian of P. Livy Larensis, a rich citizen, a descendent of Varro, and the owner of an immense library. This job furnished the scholar with a marvelous opportunity to compile, with loving care, his immense work entitled *The Deipnosophists* (*Deipnosophistae* means "learned banquet"), a treatise divided into fifteen books and dedicated to his benefactor. Within the pages of *The Deipnosophists*, we not only find the most detailed notes about ancient Greek food and cookery from the times of Homer forward, but we are also informed about how much and what was served at banquets elsewhere along the Mediterranean coast.

Indeed, the curiosity of Greek authors did not end at the shores of their sea, but extended into the far reaches of the known world. Megasthenes, a Greek author of the Hellenistic era who arrived in India following Alexander the Great, described what the Indians ate and how the food was served. In his second book, *Indika* ("History of India"), he recounts that in that far-off land a low table was set next to each guest, and on it was placed a golden bowl filled to the brim with boiled rice and a number of strongly spiced meat sauces. This shows that even in the fourth century B.C., Indian food was based on curry sauces.

Megasthenes was not the only author to write of distant peoples and their eating habits. In the many diverse texts examined by Athenaeus, authors discussed the foods and banquets of peoples from India to Spain: Celts, Germans, Thracians, Persians, ancient Syrians, Egyptians, and Parthians. They even cite the mysterious and (as far as the Greeks were concerned) utterly uncivilized Etruscans. In their writings, the Alexandrian rhetoricians and grammarians ridiculed the Phoenician habit of eating smoked fish, critiqued Ethiopian cumin, and disdained Babylonian apples; and while they commented unfavorably on the immorality of the effeminate men of Babylonia, they effused over the luxury of their dining habits. In sum, Greek writers had explored and commented on the food, cookery, gardens, farms, fisheries, leavenings, and condiments of the known world, and Athenaeus, rereading and synthesizing the texts of these writers, brought all the gastronomical facts and stories together in his anthology, a major work that is still interesting, fluid, and easy to read today.

HOMER: THE FIRST ALLUSIONS
TO FOOD AND ITS PREPARATION

Our knowledge of Greek food and eating habits begins with the Homeric poetic cycle: *The Iliad* and *The Odyssey*. Both works are of course attributed to the blind orator, Homer, but in fact they treat two distinct time periods, something that becomes abun-

dantly clear when one examines the differences in the habits of hearth and home
between the two poems.

To begin with, in The Iliad, men sat down to eat (Athenaeus 1.11 ff.), whereas the
reclining couch was used in The Odyssey; such couches were not yet known in the era
of The Iliad. In the first poem, daily life was conducted with great simplicity. At dinner
beneath the Trojan walls, the men ate chunks of beef roasted over an open fire. At this
point in history, meat was always roasted; it seems that no other cooking methods
were known. Antiphanes, a Middle Comedy poet, joked that Homer never had soup or
a bit of boiled meat prepared for his heroes. "He was so primitive," added the comic,
"that he even had tripe roasted!" Goat and lamb were also eaten, but Priam, after his
more heroic sons have died, bemoans the fact that all the offspring he has left are "the
disgraces, the liars and the dancers, . . . the plunderers of their own people in their
land of lambs and kids" (Iliad 24.261–62). In all probability he was less indignant at
their plundering than at the idea that his sons were eating food fit only for weak
females: the heroes and defenders of the country should be eating only bloody steak
and undiluted wine, comestibles that were thought to keep soldiers strong and render
them fit and keen for battle.

The heroes of the Trojan War also consumed great loaves of bread served in huge
baskets. But, according to Athenaeus, bread was never served at dinner, a meal that
consisted only of beef. As a beverage, red and even black wine was offered in expan-
sive cups—a fact that, given the environment, could be said to be heroic indeed.

Cheese is mentioned, though rarely, but in a predominantly pastoral civilization it
is only natural that cheese was made and eaten. Grated goat cheese mixed with
Pramnian wine—red, full-bodied, and heavy—was offered to the healer Machaon
by Nestor, after the former was wounded in the shoulder. This mixture was apparently
thought to give the body special sustenance: a forerunner, perhaps, of our modern
blood transfusions. To render it more palatable and tempt the wounded hero to
swallow it, Machaon was given an onion to munch between gulps of wine (Iliad
11.629–35).

Olive oil was also most important. It was then the basic seasoning for food and remained so until the end of antiquity. In ruined palaces of this period—for example, those alleged to be from the reign of Nestor at Pylos, going back thirty-three hundred years—we find traces of large *doloi* (vats) used to hold oil, as well as clay tablets in the ancient writing system of Linear B that served for bookkeeping in that remote era.

Although fish filled the Mediterranean Sea, then as now, and the people of the coast harvested it in great quantities, fish dishes are completely absent from the tables of the Trojan War heroes. It is not that Homer ignored its existence: in *The Iliad*, he describes the Hellespont as a sea abounding in fish. This fact in itself precludes the notion that not so much as a sardine was to be found on a Greek hero's table. But Homer's descriptions lack not only fish, but all fish products, as well as fruits and vegetables, although among the common people such food was surely abundantly represented at mealtimes.

It could be conjectured that such foods were not considered worthy of the mythical god-heroes, who were the stuff of legend. It is well to remember that the gods, according to mythology, dined exclusively on nectar and ambrosia; this may have led to the presumption that the heroes were nourished only by elevated foodstuffs such as beef, bread, and strong wine. There is archaeological evidence that this god-king diet was, in fact, also the choice of real kings and their courts during this historical period. In the remains of the vast Mycenaean throne rooms, or megarons—for example, those of "Agamemnon" at Mycenae and of "Nestor" at Pylos—there are signs that meat was a principal food of the royal warriors of the Bronze Age. Large, squat benches are arrayed around immense hearths, capacious enough for an entire ox; there, elbow-to-elbow, the king and his court might personally prepare their suppers while discussing government affairs. Such grand hearths were hardly the place to poach a filet of sole.

When we come to *The Odyssey*, we find that life had changed considerably since the time of *The Iliad*. According to the latest ideas, *The Odyssey* is a retelling of an eighth-century "*chanson de geste*" into which a number of later elements were incorporated. Certain habits persist: no one would have cooked and served mullet to Odysseus, for instance. Only when the beleaguered heroes face starvation, as when they are stranded in Sicily, forbidden to eat the cattle that Apollo grazed there, are they forced to eat fish (*Odyssey* 12.354–58). In fact, this Sicilian episode and the deer hunt in the Circe episode (Book 10) are the only times Odysseus and his crew resorted to fishing and hunting: no mention of fish appears elsewhere.

But in other respects, the world that *The Odyssey* describes no longer resembles that of the Trojan War. For one thing, the characters now consume their meals sprawled on the famed triclinium couches, which came into use in the late seventh to eighth century. Furthermore, the Odyssean heroes were surrounded by beautiful handmaidens and washed their hands before eating; neither of these things occurred in *The Iliad*.

Horticulture had come into use, at least at the basic level of cultivating barley and wheat. Orchards appeared, such as those found on Scheria, the land of the Phaeacians. An example is the splendid and cultivated garden of Alcinous, in which both fruit and flowers grew. In Ithaca, Odysseus's aged father, Laertes, grew his own vegetables and salad makings. The diet was more varied and although roasted meat continued to be the principal food, it was no longer the only protagonist at the banquet of this period: the monotonous and primitive carnivorous diet of earlier times had been supplanted.

A greater variety of foods began to show up even at royal tables. At the same time, cooking became more refined: after centuries of tossing everything on the fire, new ways of cooking the main dish appeared. One reads, for example, "Delicacies such as those offered to the beloved princes of Zeus," and "dainty dishes of all types"; items that could not possibly be referring to the simple, primitive pieces of bloody beef roasted on the great fireplaces of the megaron. Therefore, feasting must have become richer and more interesting, not just aimed at nourishing and strengthening the body, but also at giving pleasure to the palate and the stomach.

It is likely that many of the basic foodstuffs present in the Golden Age of Greece were already found in the homes of the Odyssean protagonists. Yet it was only in the period immediately following the sixth century that a veritable revolution in dining led to what we think of as the traditional classical meal. This dining style was to last, with slight variations, for many centuries and would constitute the most popular mode of social entertainment up to the end of classical civilization.

During the Homeric epoch, there were obviously not the sort of recipes that required a long list of ingredients and instructions: meat was thrown on the fire, in all likelihood without much added, not even a sprig of rosemary. Large baskets contained mammoth loaves of bread—unleavened, since yeast was not yet in use. It was basically a tough life, but then heroes were also tough, and doubtless they did not worry much about such trifles.

THE GOLDEN AGE BANQUET

The classic Golden Age banquet found its beginnings in the fifth century B.C. No longer was fire-roasted meat the reigning dish. Rather, fish triumphed in the kitchen, becoming the main dish: a procession of filet of bream, bass, tuna, and lobster with a vast array of mollusks: oysters, razor clams, sea urchins—as many as one could offer. This was the beginning also of the golden age of the fishmonger, who conquered the markets of the great city-states.

It is the sea's bounty that preoccupies one of the most expert gastronomes of the Hellenistic world, the Sicilian writer Archestratus of Gela. The majority of his *Hedupatheia* ("The Joys of Eating") is devoted to where to find and how to cook the best fish; a kind of early Michelin guide, giving out stars. But this is no mere recipe book or gastronomic guide: it is an epic verse, stylized in heroic hexameter, so beautiful and sonorous that Athenaeus declared the *Hedupatheia* was the only poem that wise men should cherish. What is more, it was truly useful. Before instructing the reader on how to cook a slice of tuna or make a pie out of odds and ends, Archestratus gives precious advice and outlines how to organize an elegant and lively party:
"Of learning I offer proof to all Hellas.... Let all dine at a single daintily-furnished table. There should be three or four in all, or at most not more than five. Else we should presently have a tentful of freebooters, robbers of victuals" (Athenaeus 1.4e). Then he moves on to discuss what should be presented at a meal. Above all, one

should not forget the wreaths for the guests' heads: "Always crown yourself with a wreath of all the flowers that the happy earth produces and perfume your hair with a distilled ointment."

The wreaths are not an incidental detail. We see these crowns on guests' heads, both in ancient frescoes and in every film that attempts to transport us back to the ancient world. They were an integral part of these gatherings and every guest wore one. Obviously, there were also the beautiful coronets of pure gold, now seen in museums, which were buried with their lavishly dressed owners so the latter could participate in the afterlife banquets, in which they fervently believed. But these lustrous jewels did not have the necessary curative powers that flower and leaf wreaths offered; these, when placed on one's temples, were thought to protect the wearer from the consequences of excess indulgence, due to their perfumed fragrances. It is true that such wreaths, particularly the suave, coquettish ones made of roses and violets, looked ridiculous on the heads of old judges and scowling generals, and even more so on obese politicians. They certainly looked most decorative when placed on the curls of a handsome youth or a beautiful girl. But even the old military men and fat politicians used them to calm their headaches and guard against intoxication from too much wine. One famous doctor, Triphonus, explained that the flower wreaths were not simply ornamental, but served to ward off drunkenness, migraines, and other maladies. The fresh, green ivy crown that Dionysus always wore on his head gave immediate respite from the heat of wine and even, perhaps by being pressed tightly against the temples, from headache. Roses and violets also appear to have been beneficial: roses were considered a powerful sedative, which could instantly cure the fiercest migraines. Other types of crowns might be prescribed for specific ailments: those of henna, sage, and saffron, for example, favored sleep and provided a lovely, restorative repose, allowing the wearer who had drunk too much to awake refreshed and rested. It was also important to watch out for harmful ones, such as carnations, which caused headaches, or for those made from sweet marjoram, which numbed the mind. One had to choose one's wreath wisely.

So much for the ancient "language of flowers." Appropriate wreaths were handed out to the guests at every banquet; later on, during dinner, perfumes were also dispensed.

Between flowers and perfumes, the banquet hall must have been extremely fragrant, but even this was not enough for the ancients. The day before a gathering was to take place, the dining chamber was suffused with scent. Archestratus wrote: "Continue all day long to toss myrrh and frankincense (the fruits of sweet-smelling Syria) on the soft ashes of the fire." One need only read this to understand the need for a good tight crown of ivy around the temples.

DOMESTIC DINING FROM THE FIFTH CENTURY ONWARD

We have looked at the dining habits of the heroic Mycenaean Greeks, and we have then heard the wise counsel that, nine centuries later, Archestratus gave to those wishing to organize the refined dinners that dominated the classical world. A great deal of time had passed since the Trojan War. Everything was changed; the customs were enriched and refined. There were, of course, different types of banquets; they varied according to the social and intellectual status of the participants, the host's wealth, and the customs and laws of the various parts of Greece. Many of these banquets are described in the pages of Athenaeus, from the austere dinners of philosophers to extravagant wedding feasts, from religious festivals to solemn traditions, from sedate family meals that were eaten in the gynaeceum (where the heads of families dined with mothers, wives, daughters, and close female relatives) to wild, libertine, "men-only" repasts. In short, there were meals for all tastes and incomes.

THE TRANQUIL FAMILY DINNER IN THE GYNAECEUM

We will first examine the everyday meal: the regular family dinner. There are many examples of these meals portrayed in figurative art: the men are comfortably stretched out on their triclinia, while the women are seated in chairs at the margins of the scene. In the world of Asia Minor as well as Greece, women never ate in a reclining position. For this reason, wives and girl children are always shown upright, with heads veiled, seated on chairs with high backs and armrests, sometimes with footstools. Clothing was the most correct imaginable and even the men, contentedly resting on their left elbow, were clothed from neck to toes as they dined (the ancient equivalent of wearing a coat and tie).

Typical scenes found on grave stelai are those that represent life beyond the grave as a grand, uninterrupted banquet. The eternal dinner was a ceremony restricted to the family circle; no strangers or foreigners appeared, while each and every member of the household was in attendance. Thus, entire families were depicted with their eyes fixed on the dead, each with a cup in hand, crowded into the limited space of the marble relief. At times, when the memorial stone was insufficiently large, the men of the family appear packed like sardines, while the women, deprived of space and needing the habitual chairs, appear to be perched like strange birds at one corner of the triclinium. It was imperative, however, that everyone be included within the frame and that all wives and daughters be correctly seated.

THE UNRESTRAINED BANQUETS OF MEN

Greek males generally left their wives to dine with the children while they, free from the constraints of their loved ones, indulged in the unfettered bonhomie of all-male convivial gatherings. These gatherings took place in the *andron*, a large room dedicated to this purpose that was positioned near the entrance of the androceum, the part of the house reserved for men only. The women of the house—mothers, wives, daughters, unmarried sisters—could not enter the andron for any reason whatsoever, not even to clean it when it was empty. This does not mean, however, that the dinner guests lacked female companionship.

The women who were permitted to enter the andron did so on a paid basis. They included flutists and dancers, but most importantly women of the oldest profession. These women, however, were not common street prostitutes, but rather true courtesans: refined, beautiful, and very costly. They dominated the social life of ancient Greece, playing a role similar to that of the legendary Japanese geisha. Many of them were well educated and were even permitted to attend the prestigious philosophy schools of the time. Given their beauty and high spirits, it was easy for them to establish close ties with their professors, becoming what today we might euphemistically call "friends with benefits." Such friendships generally granted them extra evening classes, where the lessons covered the most varied subject matter. By the end of their studies, these beautiful creatures would be intellectually equivalent to today's doctoral candidates, as well as adept at their most lucrative skills—those of the boudoir—for which they were justifiably famous, valued, and sought after. The richest citizens got into bidding wars over them, and many would draw up contracts for a specified time during which the chosen one agreed to accompany the man to all his dinner parties. Needless to say, she would also provide him with a prolonged after-dinner tête-à-tête. Many of these women, who had a well-honed system for padding their bills, managed to accumulate vast fortunes; wisely invested, these riches allowed them upon retirement to transform themselves into respectable philanthropists. In order to understand their importance and contributions to men's banquets, it suffices to say that Athenaeus dedicated one entire book of fifteen (Book 8) to their function, listing the first and last names and addresses of the high-ranking courtesans, and discussing the most famous among them in great detail.

The premise of these male banquets was, therefore, highly promising; the guest knew to expect a lively evening, as joyous as it was outrageous. To start with, as soon as a guest arrived, he took the liberty of shedding his clothes. Once he stretched out on the couch, he covered the lower half of his body with a light drape, but this was a mere nod to modesty since the material hid little and stirred with the minutest breeze. The courtesans did not even bother with a drape, putting their expensive merchandise on display without a trace of shame. The afternoon would unfold in the most unbridled fashion possible.

One can imagine that anything and everything might happen at these banquets, which lasted for many hours. From the beginning of the fifth century onward, dinner guests, knowing they were in for a long event, got in the habit of bringing their own "night vases" (chamber pots). Eupolis asked: "Well, then, who first said 'slave, a chamber-pot!' in the midst of his drinking?" (Athenaeus 1.17e). This custom lasted for centuries, with a few exceptions. The use of chamber pots was prohibited during certain religious festivals, such as the ritual dinner in honor of Apollo, held at Naucratis, the homeland of our own Athenaeus. They were also banned for a short time under the rule of Emperor Hadrian, but this may be ascribed to the fact that he had installed excellent sanitary facilities in his surroundings. Otherwise, commodes were always present at men's banquets. We hear mention of them right up to the end of the Roman Empire, and they may indeed have been used even longer than that. These jars, often fashioned out of precious metals, accompanied important people and emperors to their numerous banquets. In fifth century B.C. ceramics, we see them represented in guests' hands. Unfortunately, we also know that chamber pots were used for purposes other than the obvious ones. When too much wine overheated the atmosphere, and certain old arguments and puckish impulses arose, the pots made perfect projectiles for those who did not agree with the ideas being expressed. Aeschylus, in one of his satirical comedies, imagined the Homeric heroes so drunk that during a dinner they began to break their pots over each others' heads (Athenaeus 1.17c), while Sophocles, in *The Achaeans' Dinner-Guest*, wrote: "But in a burst of anger he threw the unsavoury pot, and missed not; and on my head the vessel smashed, breathing not of balsam, and the unlovely smell smote me with fright" (Athenaeus 1.17d).

We can also point to another scene common to these spectacles, often shown in figurative art and literature: that of drunken men vomiting, with the aid of a compliant handmaiden. To be far from such scenes was one benefit of the family women's circumscribed role at this time.

THE PARASITES

Besides the courtesans, musicians, and dancers—male or female—there was yet another interesting group of people at these feasts: the "parasites" or party-crashers. These were men who insinuated themselves into the feast, usually without invitation, and often found themselves without a couch, forced to sit on the floor. The parasite became a stock character at ancient Greek banquets as well as fodder for the comedies of that era. Some of these hangers-on were famous and even tolerated to a large extent, because among their characteristics were a talent for good conversation, a sharp wit, and an obliging nature. It is evident that without these gifts, such men would find themselves alone and unable to scrounge up a meal. A potential sponger, undertaking this path, had to demonstrate an exceptional sense of humor and a willingness to serve—only the clever, fun, and useful men were suffered to stay and eat. It would be a mistake to think of the Greek sponger as a figure who hovered in the background at a banquet. On the contrary, he was always visible and forward. Athenaeus dedicated a good portion of his sixth book to the most famous freeloaders of Greece, men capable of doing anything to assure admittance to a well-laden table.

He lists several by their picturesque nicknames: Tithymallus (the Greedy), Corydus (the Skylark), the Goby, the Seed Pot, the Mackerel, and the Little Mealy One (Athenaeus 6.238ff.). One was called Callimedon, otherwise known as the Lobster (or Crayfish); this one was so wildly fond of crustaceans that the Athenian fishmongers proposed erecting a bronze statue of him, eternally triumphant, clutching a lobster in his fist.

Generally if these parasites could not commandeer a spot on a couch, they were not above sitting at the feet of a guest, a practice common enough that in one comedy we witness a young man of good connections being ambushed by a freeloader while he was reclining at a banquet. The poor youth tries to shake the intruder off, using every excuse he can think of: the banquet is all but finished, he says, and besides there is absolutely no space on his couch for anyone else. But the parasite is not to be discouraged. Without a trace of embarrassment, he says, "Not to worry: that's not important in the least. In any case," he concludes cheerfully, "I'm a footstool kind of guy."

DISTINCTIVE DINNERS

Plato's Dinners: Logically, there were also literary suppers, as there are in every age. Dinners among philosophers, limited to men only, were different from those described above, as one might expect. They were certainly full of intellectual merit, to be sure, but one gets the sense that they were hardly sparkling.

Plato wrote in *The Republic* (372c) of the sort of dinner that the ideal citizens of the future might share, an austere meal notably lacking in meat and fish. When his companion Glaucon remarks that it seemed that they were to be served no relishes at their austere meals, Plato contradicts him: they would be given such delicacies as salt, olives (Recipe 6), and cheese, as well as *lampascioni*, the wild hyacinth bulbs that needed a great deal of artifice to help them lose their bitter flavor and render them edible (Recipe 9). The meal, Plato assured Glaucon, was to be finished off with treats such as figs, chickpeas, and fava beans. Sated with such gastronomical treats, the guests would pass their time after dinner, seated around the fire, roasting myrtle berries and acorns, while they sipped, obviously in great moderation, watered wine. What more could one ask of life?

Cynics at Supper: Continuing in the realm of philosophers, we have a description of another, equally sumptuous banquet given by Parmeniscus the Cynic. The dinner was held at the home of Cebes of Cyzicus, during the feast of Dionysos in Athens (Athenaeus 4.156–58). From what we understand, there were nine participants. Besides Parmeniscus, there was the owner of the house, plus six cynics, and Carneius of Megara.

To start, rivers of lentil soup were served (Recipe 15). They had barely finished it when another type of lentil soup arrived (Recipe 16); next came lentils seasoned with vinegar. At this point, one of the guests, being a Cynic and therefore feeling entitled to despise the shabbiness of life, had reached the end of his patience. Jumping to his feet, with his hands upraised to the heavens, he prayed that Zeus would punish the knave responsible for drowning them in lentils. Twisting the knife further, all present—except the host, who was responsible for the misdeed, and one guest—joined in the prayer. One Cynic, however, came to the defense of the lowly lentil, chiding a fellow guest named Plutarch (not the historian Plutarch of a later century): "Yet, you men of fair Alexandria, Plutarch, have been brought up on lentil food, and your entire city is full of lentil dishes" (Athenaeus 4.158d). Certainly true, but probably also the reason why poor Plutarch had had enough of them.

Indeed, one should not belittle the lentil: this greatly economical legume played a major role in feeding the less well-off. It seems that the only drawback was the nasty smell that lingered on the eater's breath, which some apparently (or perhaps apocryphally) tried to ameliorate by adding fragrances. Strattis of Phoenicia gave these words to his character Jocasta: "I wish to give you two some wise advice; when you make lentil-soup don't pour in perfume" (Athenaeus 4.160c). Regarding fragrance in lentil soup, there was even a Greek proverb, used when one wanted to indicate that something has gone amiss. Thus, in a theatrical piece by Sopater, a character exclaims, "Odysseus of Ithaca is here; as the saying goes, the perfume is in the soup. Have courage, my soul!" In any case, lentil soup may have made for bad breath, but it served the purpose of filling the stomach, and a lentil soup is always very tasty. Let us not forget that Esau transferred his birthright to Jacob for a plate of lentils.

WEDDING BANQUETS

Of all the types of banquets, the wedding banquet was the most joyous and free from restrictions, and we will present a pair of examples. One describes the wedding dinner of a miser, while the other exemplifies a marriage feast given by a very wealthy member of a royal family, as open-handed as the miser was penurious.

In the comedy *Unveiling of the Bride* (Kock 3.376; Athenaeus 14.644d–e), Euangelus presents the miserly head of house as he orders his slave about:

> *Father:* I told you to set four tables for the women and six for the men; the dinner
> is to be complete, and not a thing must be lacking. We want the wedding to be
> a brilliant one. You don't need to ask questions of anyone else; I'll tell you every-
> thing, keeping my eye on you the while. As to the fish, you shall buy all the kinds
> you like; for the meat courses you have got veal, young sows, suckling-pigs, hares.
> *Cook's boy* (aside): What a braggart this damned fellow is!
> *Father:* Platter of fig-leaves [Recipe 12], cheese, moulded cakes.
> *Cook:* Boy there, Dromon!
> *Father:* A Lydian sauce, some eggs, a nice meal-cake . . .

The wedding feast hosted by Caranus was an entirely different sort of affair, a banquet served according to the customs of Alexander the Great's homeland. In that country, the bride and groom received gifts from friends, but the host also gave gifts to the guests. This custom persisted into the 1900s, in Greece and elsewhere: guests at a ball or a grand dinner always left with a souvenir. But the gifts parceled out to the partici-pants at Caranus's banquet were no mere trinkets.

Twenty guests—a select and aristocratic group—came to this little feast, which was destined to go down in history. Everything about it was noteworthy and extraordinary, and it was described in great detail in Athenaeus's fourth book: the luxurious furnish-ings, the richness of the foods and wines, the entertainment that brightened the meal, and, above all, the gifts offered to the guests. The distribution of these trifles began immediately; indeed, the guests had barely sprawled on their couches when each received a gift of a silver cup, as well as a golden crown of inestimable value that was placed on the guest's head upon arrival. The rain of precious gifts seemed never to cease: having barely emptied their cups, they were each offered a bronze Corinthian tray, completely covered with a large loaf of bread. Artfully placed on top of the bread were chickens, ducks, doves, geese, and every kind of meat. Each guest accepted his tray of food and, after tasting the delicacies, passed them on to their attendant slaves.

Then the next course was served, and each guest was presented with another large platter, this time in silver and covered with a focaccia (Recipe 1), on which were displayed roast kid goats (Recipe 21), geese, specially and individually designed sandwiches, then pigeons, doves, partridges, and other wild game. Once again, after the guests sampled these dishes, they were passed on to the slaves. When the guests had eaten their fill, they washed their hands.

At this point, each guest was offered a floral crown, but to render the gift more lasting, each was also given another golden crown, as heavy and valuable as the first. Then came various toasts. The guests were overwhelmed by the excitement, and even more so when the flutists, singers, and Rhodian sambuca players entered. The girls appeared to be naked, but may merely have been dressed in very transparent tunics. When the flutists left, a succession of new girls arrived, each carrying two jars, one silver, the other gold, held together by a golden band and containing a liter of perfume. These also were given to the guests. After this, huge, heavy, gold-plated silver trays arrived, each bearing a pig stuffed with all sorts of delicacies: thrushes, ducks, warblers, wheat polenta with egg, oysters, and periwinkles. As always, each guest was given his own tray and his own pig. Then followed boiled kid goat on precious plates for each to take home, in addition to golden spoons.

Just then, as the guests asked themselves how they could manage to carry home such an array of gifts, Caranus ordered his servants to give his friends baskets and chests for the bread; the chests were fashioned from thin strips of ivory. The delighted guests applauded. Immediately, another gold crown and more perfumes in jars arrived, just as costly as the previous gifts. Then followed the most lively entertainment, ithyphallic dancers (in honor of Dionysos), clowns, and nude acrobats, who performed with the sharpest of swords while spouting fire from their mouths.

The party was not yet over. It continued in grand style: gifts of gold cups and wines from Thasos, Mende, and Lesbos were passed out, immediately followed by a crystal platter for each guest. This platter was two cubits (80 cm) in diameter and was supported beneath by a silver tray, full of every type of fish and seafood imaginable (Recipes 26–49) With it came yet more silver baskets, with loaves of Capadocian bread. When the guests had eaten a morsel, they passed the rest to the slaves. Again, they washed their hands, and, truly pampered, were presented with yet another golden cup, this one twice as heavy and valuable as the others. With it came another double vase of perfumes for each guest.

They began to drink in earnest. One of the guests called for a gallon-sized cup, had it filled with Thasian wine with barely a drop of water added, and promptly drank it down, saying, "The more one drinks, the fewer one's woes." Caranus, full of admiration for this feat, gave him the cup and offered to do the same for any who followed suit. All tried and succeeded except for one. The failure sat and wept at his lack of success, but his host consoled him by giving him a cup anyway.

Meanwhile, the entertainment continued as a hundred-man chorus sang a wedding song, followed by dancers dressed as Nereids and nymphs. Time passed pleasantly and night fell. Suddenly, the white linen curtains that surrounded the room flew open. The amazed guests were treated to a remarkable scene: against the dark background of the garden, statues appeared representing Cupids, Dianas, Pans, and Hermae, and each held a lit torch. As the guests marveled at this sight, they were each served a large wild boar laced up with silver filigree and arrayed on a square, golden platter. For whatever reason, either the beauty of the presentation or the gift itself, this last and most unexpected gift put all the guests into the highest of spirits. Meanwhile, the slaves started to prepare for the return home, packing the gifts into the ivory chests. The guests only awaited the Macedonian custom of trumpets heralding the close of the banquet. Yet, still they drank, but now from small cups, while a comedian entertained them. Finally, more ivory chests arrived, this time with desserts—sweets of all types from Cretan to

Samian—each presented in an elegant box, much as sugared almonds are doled out at today's Italian and Greek weddings. The guests, grateful and overjoyed, bid their host good-bye, wishing him the best from the bottom of their hearts.

It is no surprise, then, to hear that Hippolochus the Macedonian, one of the guests, gave a detailed account of the banquet in a letter to his friend Lynceus, who had had to stay behind in Athens (Athenaeus 4.128–130d). The former teased the latter saying that while Lynceus remained at Athens to celebrate the Lenaean festival, eating the traditional feast day bread, flavored with arugula and thyme, Hippolochus and his fellow guests "have carried away a fortune from Caranus's banquet instead of trifling portions, and are now looking for houses or lands or slaves to buy."

GREEK MENUS

Certainly not all meals were wedding feasts, and the fare offered at a cheery dinner for friends would be less elaborate. Regardless of the size of the meal, it was generally important to be mindful of expenses.

A DELICIOUS YET ECONOMICAL MENU
The fourth–third century poet Alexis, in *Crateus*, or *The Apothecary*, gives us an example of what, during his time, would have been considered a simple menu, as well as one to offer on the spur of the moment to those defined in Greek as "friends of salt and beans"; that is to say, those intimate friends who would share a meal of just beans and a bit of salt. In this comedy, one of the characters lists what he finds at the market to prepare for such a meal:

> First, then, I spied oysters, wrapped in seaweed, in the shop of an Old Man of the
> Sea, and sea-urchins too [Recipe 8]; I grabbed them; for they are the prelude to
> a daintily ordered dinner. Next, I came upon some little fish, all trembling for
> fear of what was to happen to them. But I bade them have no fears as far as I was
> concerned, promising that I wouldn't harm a single one, and bought a large
> greyfish. Then I took an electric ray-fish [Recipe 38], being mindful that when
> a lady lays tender fingers upon it she must not suffer any hurt from its thorny

touch. For the frying-pan I got some wrasse, sole, shrimp, jack hake, gudgeon, perch, and sea-bream, and made the dish gayer than a peacock. Then came some meats—feet, snouts, and swines' ears [Recipe 19], and liver wrapped in caul; for it is ashamed of its own livid color. No professional cook shall come near these, or even look upon them. He will rue it, let me tell you. Rather, I shall myself act as steward, so cleverly, so smoothly, and elegantly (yes, I shall make the dish myself), that I shall cause the feasters now and then to push their teeth into the plates for very joy. The preparation and composition of all these foods I am ready to disclose, proclaim, and teach for nothing if anybody wishes to learn. (Kock 2.233; Athenaeus 3.107)

Thus, we have a menu consisting of a seafood antipasto, boiled or roasted fish, fried fish, a mixed grill, and, finally, a bit of liver in a net. What's more, we find a generous cook, willing to share his secrets.

A DELUXE DINNER

Sometimes a host spared no expense and filled the table with an unending variety of dishes. From what we have read, we note that a Greek banquet between the fifth and fourth centuries B.C. was an extremely serious dining experience, with so many and such a variety of offerings that even if one merely tasted what was offered, one would have to have a superhuman appetite to reach the end. Philoxenus of Cythera in a play called *The Banquet* (PLG 3.601; Athenaeus 4.146–47) lists more than thirty-five courses. Even if many of these servings consisted of bread, sandwiches, or focaccia, the list of offerings was enough to make even Gargantua and Pantagruel blanch.

And slaves twain brought unto us a table with well-oiled face, another for others, while other henchmen bore a third, until they filled the chamber. The tables glistened in the rays of the high-swinging lamps, freighted with trenchers and condiments delectable in cruets, full . . . and luxuriant in divers artful inventions to pleasure life, tempting lures of the spirit. Some slaves set beside us snowy-topped barley cakes in baskets, while others (brought in loaves of wheat). After them first came not an ordinary tureen, my love, but a riveted vessel of huge size; . . . a glistening dish of eels to break our fast, full of conger-faced morsels

18

that would delight a god [Recipe 31]. After this another pot of the same size came in, and a soused ray of perfect roundness. There were small kettles, one containing some meat of a shark [Recipe 35], another a sting-ray [Recipe 30]. Another rich dish there was, made of squid and sepia-polyps with soft tentacles [Recipe 47]. After this came a grey mullet hot from its contact with fire, the whole as large as the table, exhaling spirals of steam. After this came breaded squid, my friend, and cooked prawns done brown. Following these we had flower-leaved cakes and fresh confections spiced, puff-cakes of wheat with frosting, large as the pot. This is called the "navel of the feast" by you and me. Last there came—the gods are my witnesses—a monstrous slice of tunny [tuna], baked hot, from over the sea where it was carved with knives from the meatiest part of the belly [Recipe 32].

Philoxenus continues his description of the meats and others courses served, so numerous that the poet lost count, listing them one after the other in an interminable catalog: entrails, tripe, loin, and leg of domestic pig, kid goats cut in half, the legs, feet, ribs and head of a pig (Recipes 24 and 25), and a filet flavored with silphium (an extinct plant also used medicinally). Nor did it stop there, because the narrator states that when these morsels were gone, the containers were withdrawn and replaced by others: "Kid and lamb, boiled and roast, and sweetest morsel of under-done entrails from kids and lambs mixed, such as the gods love, . . . jugged hare, and young cockerels, and many hot portions of partridge and ring-doves were now lavishly laid beside us. Loaves of bread there were, light and nicely folded; and companioning there came in also yellow honey and curds, and as for cheese. . . ." And with this, and thankfully, the banquet ended and the guests washed their hands.

Large amounts of food, but one does not hear mention of any vegetables, either cooked or raw, nor sweets or fruits, even though these existed and were consumed in good quantity. From citations of fifth-century Greek authors we have a record of which fruits and vegetables were sold in the Greek market of the era.

All Greeks gathered together to feast, but they did not eat the same things nor did they eat in the same style everywhere. Greece, in fact, was divided into its numerous city-states, each politically and economically independent of—and often enemies with—all the others. This independence extended to the arena of gastronomy and the rules for producing one's banquets. We read in Diphilus's *The Woman Who Left Behind Her Husband* (quoted in Athenaeus 4.133c; Kock 2.545) that the cook, before choosing a menu, asked where the guests were from. The head of the house impatiently asked what the devil difference it would make, upon which the chef explained that there were different tastes and manners in the various cities of Greece and that to be able to please the guests, he needed to know where they came from. Thus, we learn that the people of Rhodes above all loved eating "large sheat-fish" (shad?) or a lebias (an unidentified fish) and they expected it to be served hot. In Byzantium, on the other hand, they made everything into soup and seasoned it with quantities of absinthe (bitters), garlic, and salt.

Menander in his *Trophonius* (again, quoted in Athenaeus 4.132e; Kock 3.132) repeats this information. In this comedy, when discussing what to offer a foreigner for dinner, one of the speakers said that one had to know where a guest came from because it would make a difference to the chef. For example, those coming from the Greek islands were accustomed to eating a great deal of fish of all kinds, but they ate it fresh, out of the sea, and were therefore "not at all attracted to preserved fish." If they were obliged to eat it that way, they would do so unwillingly; they would prefer "force-meats and highly seasoned dishes." The Arcadians, on the other hand, perhaps because they lived far from the sea, were fascinated with anything marine, especially bivalves, while the Ionians appreciated only hearty, rich foods "that provoke desire."

These remarks make sense if one understands that each city made a show of disapproving all that pertained to its rivals, and that each city made fun of the others. Regional critiques, above all those made by the comedic dramatists, were not just based on the customs of each *polis* but also on the characteristics of its citizens. These jabs could be highly entertaining and everyone took part, laughing at the Athenians, the Spartans, the Thebans, and even the Greek colonials of Syracuse and Tarantum alike. Each jest centered on the regional characteristics, the preferred food choices, and the vices and caprices of each group, and no one was spared. Let us examine these in quick succession, starting with mythic Athens, the cradle of civilization and art.

ATHENS

The Athenian menu was the butt of many dramatists' jokes. From their writings, we know that it was composed of a series of bite-sized tastes, diverse but small. This custom persists even today. One needs only to go to Plaka and ask for ouzo, the anise-flavored Greek liquor, to find that one gets a series of little bites with the drink, the number and quality of the offerings depending on the level of the establishment. Even into the recent past, Greek law prohibited establishments from serving ouzo without also serving food. I remember an open-air locale in remotest Crete, where the tables were left over from the last war—huge, round barrels that once held fuel for the American fleet. There, seated under the stars, we ordered glasses of ouzo and watched as the waiter arrived, staggering under the weight of a large tray, where, besides our aperitif, there were numerous plates heaped with such foods as the Greek comedic dramatists wrote about twenty-five hundred years ago. The menu had not changed since the age of Pericles. It was a delicious way to pass an afternoon, but it was certainly not a meal to satisfy. Nevertheless, this repast, today part of the Greek aperitif, if multiplied several times over, would have constituted the entire ancient Athenian meal.

Clearly one can assume a bit of exaggeration on the part of the comic writers, and probably such skimpy fare was more characteristic of ancient eateries than private homes. But for those who did not own a home, this was what the market offered and the comedian Alexis from Tunis, in his *Running Mates* (Athenaeus 4.137c–d), had it said to one of his characters that he ought to hire the two best cooks in the city, because, intending to invite a guest from Thessaly, he did not want to expose said guest to the typical Athenian offerings: "I must not stretch the gentleman on the rack of famine by stingily setting before him each little dish separately."

Along the same lines, Lynceus, in *The Centaur*, makes fun of Athenian dinners and their numerous minute portions, so small that they would not even be shared with a friend:

Patron: For the cook sets before you a large tray on which are five small plates. One of these holds garlic, another a pair of sea-urchins, another a sweet wine sop, another ten cockles, the last a small piece of sturgeon. While I am eating this, another is eating that; and while he is eating that, I have made away with this. What I want, good sir, is both the one and the other, but my wish is impossible. For I have neither five mouths nor five right hands. Such a lay-out as that seems to offer variety, but it is nothing at all to satisfy the belly. For I simply bespatter my lips, I don't fill them. What, then, have you?

Cook: A lot of oysters.

Patron: You serve me a plate of them, all by itself, and not a small one, either. Have you sea-urchins?

Cook: Yes, of these you shall have a second course. For I bought them myself, fourpence (8 obols) worth.

Patron: This then is the one dish you shall serve by itself, that all may eat it alike— not I one thing, my companion another (Athenaeus 4.131f–132c; Kock 3.274).

Given these examples, it does not seem likely that Athenians ate well. In fact, several authors portray the Athenian dinner as even worse than that of the austere Spartans. It depended, moreover, on the historical moment that the author wrote about. The low point in Athenian dining was probably under the rule of Solon (sixth–seventh century B.C.), a harsh legislator who set strict limits on every form of luxury. He even wrote that one should only serve economical, rustic barley bread at dinner: wheat bread was condoned only on special occasions. Solon did not stop there: he imposed on the citizens an absolute prohibition on the purchase of imports. His fellow citizens took him at his word; they not only observed his laws, but carried them to the point of absurdity. Chrysippus in his tract *On Pleasure and Good* (Athenaeus 4.137f) recounts that in the lyceum and the academy there were two traditional banquets held every year. Once, a cook for one of these feasts dared to carry in a casserole dish destined for some other use, and the indignant sufferers, believing that the cook was guilty of smuggling, broke the dish into pieces. Apparently this food dish represented the sort of extravagance that Solon had banned, though what could be seen as "extravagant" about a baking dish remains a mystery today. Certainly it was more reprehensible when a cook, in preparing a dinner, playfully fashioned some salted meat to look like a fish. This cook was flogged "for playing the impostor with his over-refinement."

SPARTA

The Spartans were always the preferred target of all types of comedians. Even today, when this city is mentioned, one thinks of the strict laws drafted by Lycurgus, the harsh Spartan life style, and the famous and infamous communal table, the only place at which Spartan males might take their meals. Obligatory dining, yes, but not free; in fact the communal table had nothing whatsoever to do with modern ideas of a social or welfare state. There was no help for those who did not work and could not be useful to the community. It was mandated that equal portions were given to all at meals and it was further required that all participants would cover the expenses for the maintenance and upkeep of the communal table. Everyone contributed equally, giving seventy-eight liters of barley, forty-two liters of wine, plus a certain quantity of cheese and figs, and it was also expected that each pay the sum of ten Egyptian obols toward the purchase of meat. Men could add something extra, as a gift to the community, but it could not be purchased goods: only animals they had raised or game they had captured themselves. Those with flocks gave lamb and goats; others gave ringdoves, geese, turtledoves, thrushes, blackbirds, or rabbits. The cook, when serving these offerings, announced the name of the one who donated it, and the donor probably received a well-deserved round of applause for his patriotism.

The daily fare was plain and sparse. It was listed in full by Dicaearchus in his *Tripoliticus* (FGH 2.242; Athenaeus 4.141b): barley bread, a slice of boiled pork that could not weigh more than an *etto* (one quarter of a pound), to which was added the broth from boiling the meat, and sometimes they even had olives (Recipe 6), cheese, and some figs, and whatever roasted meat the donors brought. On top of this, they drank a cup of wine.

At the end of this delicious repast, the young boys were given an extra bit of food, financed by the wealthiest citizens, while the poor were compensated by being allowed to take a portion of reeds or straw to reinforce their dwellings. The boys' extra ration of food consisted of barley flour (imagine something like polenta), flavored with oil, and the young boys avidly ate it with an added bay leaf. Chewing bay leaves at the end of a meal was a pleasure not just reserved for the youth, but an ancient Greek habit. Callias (or Diocles) wrote, in *The Cyclopians*: "Here come the dish of leaves, which means an end to our dinners and our dances as well" (Athenaeus 4.140e). (Who would be able to dance on such a diet will always remain a mystery.) Today it seems truly strange that the tough bay leaf would be an attractive dessert, but back then they picked it clean.

Often these Spartan communal meals were dominated by a famous black soup—a local specialty as characteristic of Sparta as pizza is of Naples and saffron-flavored risotto is of Milan. This dark soup seems to have had a disagreeable flavor. As Plutarch relates in his life of Lycurgus, a certain king of Pontus wanted to sample this soup and he sent for a Spartan chef to prepare it. The king had barely put the spoon in his mouth when he grimaced with disgust. The cook let it be known that it was not his fault that the monarch did not like the soup: "Sir, to make this broth relish, you should have bathed yourself first in the river Eurotas," that is, in Sparta's river. It seems that the rest of the Spartans not only swallowed this soup, but ate it with pleasure and added their bread to it, turning it black as coal.

Besides their food, Spartans were also pilloried for their rusticity and ignorance. Exemplary of such sport is the tale of a Spartan who, finding himself in a more refined city, was invited to a sumptuous supper. The antipasto platter was heaped with foods completely unknown to him, including beautiful sea urchins (Recipe 8). The unschooled youth took one and, in front of his surprised, amused, and incredulous fellow guests, put the whole sea urchin in his mouth: egg, shell, sharp spines, and all. Naturally, with his first bite, he found himself in an awkward position, but, being a Spartan, he could not falter. Struggling to keep his composure, he continued to chew the wicked thing until he destroyed it completely. Triumphant, though in agony, he declared: "You malicious animal. You did not get me. I won, me! But one thing is certain, in the future I will never eat another sea urchin." Never was a vow more truly respected.

24

THEBES

Thebans were said to be the most tight-fisted of the Greeks and their meals were described as truly miserable. The historian Cleitarchus, in the first book of his history of Alexander, relates that when Thebes was destroyed by that king, the city's collective wealth was less than 440 talents. Perhaps this was the reason for their frugal meals. Their suppers were scraped together from *thrion* (stuffed fig leaves) (Recipe 12), cooked vegetables, anchovies, little fish (Recipe 29), sausages, ox ribs, and bean porridge. This was exactly what Attaginus, son of Phrynon, served to the Persian Mardonius and fifty of his military men, when the former invited them to his house. Cleitarchus wrote gleefully: "I believe that [the Persians] could not have won the battle, and that the Greeks need not have met them in battle-array at Plataea, seeing that they already had been done to death by the food" (Athenaeus 4.148d–f).

GREATER GREECE: TARANTUM

In Tarantum (modern Taranto) on the Italian coast, by contrast, life was quite agreeable and the food was excellent. The Tarantans did not bother pinching pennies and they partied every day. Once a month public sacrifices were made and the victims' roasted meat was eaten, but even on other days the people were not particularly penitent and private citizens produced succulent dinners. The Tarantans felt that, while other men considered it necessary to amass riches to allow them to live in luxury someday, Tarantans did not waste time: "they themselves, with their parties and their pleasures, do not put off living, but live already" (Athenaeus 4.166e–f).

HELLENISM AND ALEXANDER THE GREAT

With Alexander the Great (356–368 B.C.), one enters the Hellenistic era and an extravagant and rich world. In fact, not much is known about the dietary habits of Alexander except for his passion for apples, especially those from Babylonia (Athenaeus 7.276f–277a). This youth was a warrior: young, good-looking, strong and capable of enduring hunger and thirst without turning a hair, but also one who was driven to the worst excesses, even when he was still a boy. This is demonstrated by the battle of the apples, in which Alexander and his friends filled their boat with the fruit, shoved off, and using them as projectiles, improvised a lively battle. No one died, but there were plenty of wounds.

Alexander may have loved good, healthy apples, but he also loved a less innocuous item: wine. It is said he drank it pure and in huge quantities, often ending up thoroughly drunk. This vice was blamed for both his early death and his sexual indifference—a failing that, however, did not preclude him from marrying Roxane, Oxyartes' daughter, and fathering a child by her. Nevertheless, when Alexander moved to Asia, he left his wife behind, but he permitted his men's mistresses to sup and drink with their menfolk. It was at one of these drunken, mixed-gender entertainments that Ptolemy's celebrated Athenian mistress, Thais, convinced Alexander to set fire to Xerxes' palace.

There were a great many magnificent banquets in Alexander's life. Sometimes so many people were invited that there was not enough room for them all to repose on couches, and the guests ended up sitting. But even in these cases—as, for example, at the banquet serving over six thousand officials—the meals were splendid and the guests had seats made of silver. The expenses for dinners that he offered his friends were fantastically high: more than one hundred minas were expended to feed sixty or seventy people. Given that a mina was worth roughly 4,333 kilos of silver, the cost per guest was about 62–72 kilos of silver.

Alexander's friends were no less extravagant and they showed it above all when they invited the young conqueror to dine. Agatharchides of Cnidus in his *Asian Affairs* (FGH 3.196) tells us that one such host had all the desserts wrapped in gold leaf. Every time the guests took one, they peeled off and tossed the gold on the floor with the other garbage to show their admiration for such extravagance. No doubt the slaves profited from this display of casual extravagance as they took out the deluxe garbage.

EXPENSES

Needless to say, the average person did not spend as freely on his entertainments as did Alexander. Menander, in his comic play *Drunkenness* (or *The Carouse*), calculates that a large banquet cost about one talent (Allinson 402; Athenaeus 4.146 d–e): "So then, our prosperity accords not with the way in which we offer sacrifice. For though to the gods I bring an offering of a tiny sheep bought for ten drachmas [equivalent to 4–4.5 g of silver, or U.S. $7–8], and glad I am to get it so cheap; but for flute-girls and perfume, harp-girls, Mendean and Thasian wine, eels, cheese, and honey, the cost is almost a talent [6,000 drachmas]." Menander specifies neither the number of guests nor the type of banquet, but a talent (26 kg of silver) would be roughly equivalent to four or five thousand U.S. dollars. Even today, for a reception or dinner for 100 to 150 guests, one could spend about this amount—without, naturally, the girl-flutists, girl-harpists, or fragrances. I would say that a well-heeled host of today would comprehend these prices and see them as a comparable outlay.

Innkeepers' food bills, often horribly inflated, were the subject of jokes then as now. In a comedy called *The Man with a Cataract* (*Apeglaucomenos*) by Alexis (Kock 2.366; Athenaeus 3.117), we see a customer who refuses to pay his share of a social lunch if the innkeeper does not justify the bill line by line. The scene seems to demonstrate that at such gatherings there are those who use the group's good faith to profit themselves, as well as those who are naturally mistrustful.

[Customer]: If ... you don't render me an account of each item in detail, you
shall not get from me a twelfth part of a farthing.
[Owner]: What you say is reasonable. Bring a counting-board and counters.
[Customer]: Name the items.
[Owner]: Raw salt fish, five farthings [obols].
[Customer]: Next!
[Owner]: Mussels, seven farthings.
[Customer]: You haven't cheated yet. Next!
[Owner]: Those sea urchins, a ha'penny [1 obol].
[Customer]: Your conscience is still clean.
[Owner]: After that wasn't there the cabbage which you all loudly praised?
[Customer]: Yes; it was really good.
[Owner]: I paid a penny for that.
[Customer]: Why, I wonder, were we so loud in praising it?
[Owner]: The cube salt-fish cost three ha'pence.

[Customer]: A bargain, indeed! And for the endive you haven't charged a single penny!

[Owner]: You don't know, simpleton, the state of the market, and that the weevil have eaten up all green salads.

[Customer]: So that's why you have charged double for the salt-fish?

[Owner]: The fishmonger is to blame; go and ask him. Next come the conger eel, five pence [10 obols].

[Customer]: That's not much! Name the next.

[Owner]: I bought the baked fish for a shilling.

[Customer]: Ow! Like a fever—it leaves one, then rises high again.

[Owner]: Add the wine, of which I procured more when you were drunk; three bottles, at five pence [10 obols] the bottle.

WINE AND THE SYMPOSIUM

According to myth, grapevines, and consequently wine, were the gifts of Dionysos. This god hailed from Egypt, where vineyards were already under cultivation by 4000 B.C. At some point Dionysos sailed for Greece, carrying the precious grapevine with him. Legend holds that during the journey, the divine ship was waylaid by pirates, who bound the handsome young god in chains. Only the pilot of the pirate ship recognized the supernatural radiance of the captive, and he begged his companions not to offend the solitary sailor, but in vain. So much the worse for them: Dionysos burst his chains and turned the offending pirates into dolphins. Archaeologists have unearthed a beautiful ceramic cup from the sixth century B.C. representing this myth: the god steers the ship, whose main mast is twined with a huge vine hanging with grapes, while the pirate-dolphins leap in the waves. Thus Dionysos came to the shores of Greece and introduced his plant and his wine.

Men took such a liking to this beverage, far stronger than today's wine, that they soon began to poison themselves with it. Greek authors relate that many early imbibers ended up dead, crazy, or alcoholic under the influence of pure wine. Herodotus wrote that the Spartan king Cleomenes, having lived among the Scythians, a savage population devoted to strong drink and therefore to drunkenness, had begun to drink like these savages and gradually went mad from it (*History* 6.84). Thereafter, every time the Spartans wanted to be served something stronger, they ordered the wine merchant to "make it like the Scythians" (Athenaeus 10.427b–c). There were many who "drank like Scythians," not the least of whom was the young hero Alexander the Great (10.434c–d).

Soon after wine was introduced, man had already begun to abuse it and act like madmen. It was only when man learned to dilute the wine that it became as safe as it was pleasing. The ancient writers gave several different explanations for how wine came to be diluted. According to one version, expounded by Philonides in his work *Perfumes and Wreaths* (Athenaeus 15.675a–c), Zeus himself intervened to save the alcoholics. One day, a group of men were drinking strong wine by the sea when a sudden storm, sent by Zeus, burst upon them. They fled to a nearby cave, leaving the remains of their picnic behind on the beach. When the storm was over, the men found that the rain had filled their half-empty wine goblets. This watered wine, they found, was not only good to drink but above all better for them. From then on, at the beginning of a symposium or wine-drinking ceremony, each guest was given a mouthful of pure wine to salute Dionysos, the giver of wine: but thereafter, as they began to drink diluted wine, they thanked Zeus the Savior.

In another version, the Athenian king Amphictyon learned the method from Dionysos himself. The king thereafter erected a statue to an "upright" (that is, not falling-down drunk) Dionysos at the Temple of the Seasons (Athenaeus 2.38c–d) and near this statue he installed an altar to the Nymphs, who are called "the wet nurses of Dionysos," to remind the devotees that wine should be tempered with water. Quoted Athenaeus, "In daily intercourse, to those who mix and drink [wine] moderately, it gives good cheer; but if you overstep the bounds, it brings violence" (2.36a).

It was, therefore, with diluted wine that Greeks finished their banquets and began the symposium. This classic after-dinner festivity of snacking and wine-drinking began with the election of a "symposiarch," a sort of master of ceremonies, part psychologist and part social director. A good symposium facilitator was essential to an evening's success. He was supposed to help strengthen existing friendships among the guests and inspire new ones. He was to keep firm control of the conversation and head off contentious turns. Finally, the symposiarch was arbiter of the number of toasts and the dilution of the wine. It was best if the elected one had first-class medical knowledge, so that he might calculate how the wine would affect the diverse guests: the aim was that no one should get so drunk that arguments and disorder ensued.

Various calculations were used for diluting wine: a formula of half water and half wine was judged to be too dangerous (Athenaeus 10.426a). Other common dilutions were the "five" (three parts water to two parts wine); the "three" (two parts water to one of wine); and finally, the "four" (three parts water to one of wine). But everyone, Plutarch included, found that this last formula made the wine too weak a drink, and only good for wise judges (or so the story goes).

The symposium leader needed to ensure that the number of toasts did not exceed the number of emptied cups. According to Athenaeus, the temperate person limited himself to three diluted cups: one for the toast, one for love, and one for dreams. At that point, the smart man went home. Those who stayed longer knew that the fourth cup led to violence, the fifth to rowdiness, the sixth to happy drunkenness, the seventh to laughter (the Greeks called this "to black eyes"), the eighth to policeman, the ninth to biliousness, and the tenth to insanity and the smashing of furniture (Athenaeus 1.36b–c).

One story tells of a group of young men from Agrigentum who had surely arrived at the tenth cup and probably did not stop there. This group gathered one day for dinner and began to drink without restraint. After a while, the world began to spin about them and they somehow could not get to their feet. They seized upon the notion that they were on a trireme caught in a terrible storm and that the only way to avoid shipwreck was to lighten the boat. Staggering to their feet, they began to throw the furniture out the window. Naturally the racket drew a crowd, which wasted no time in making off with the items flung onto the street.

When the authorities came on the scene to investigate, they found the lads still under the influence and still convinced that they were on an imperiled trireme. Moreover, the arrival of the strangers, striding across what seemed to the tipplers to be a sea of tossing waves, convinced them that they were in the presence of supernatural beings. Befuddled as they were, they could only say that the marine tempest was wreaking havoc on their ship and to save themselves they had been obliged to jettison the excess cargo. Turning respectfully to the speechless magistrates, one youth explained, "Honorable Tritons, I was so frightened that I went to hide in the hold and I have not moved from there."

The magistrates realized there was no point in arguing and they began to depart. But before they reached the door, the young men prostrated themselves at the elders' feet, solemnly swearing that if they were suffered to escape this terrible storm and make port, they would raise an altar in honor of these, their savior sea gods. After this episode, the house was forevermore known as "the Trireme."

This tale serves to illustrate how important it was that the symposiarch be very attentive to both the dilution of the wine and the number of toasts. A certain number of toasts were obligatory. But in those days, toasts were not made in honor of present company; they were made in honor of the gods or, as often as not, some personage whom everyone admired. Theophrastus writes in his treatise on drunkenness that because in antiquity it was not customary to toast the health of another, it was by means of the "kottabos" that lovers found a way to honor their beloved. Kottabos was a drinking game, in which the dregs of a cup were flung at a target, usually a plate. According to Theophrastus:

> Initially one toasted the gods only. In those days the kottabos was the tool by
> which lovers honored each other. In fact, they were assiduously devoted to this
> game, about which Anacreon of Teos wrote: "With hands tied together we play
> the Sicilian kottabos" [PLG fr. 53]. From then on, all of the ancient poems that we
> call "skolia" (cheerful group songs) are full of references [to this game]; I refer
> to the poems that Pindar composed (PLG 441). "... [T]he pleasure of love is
> inspired by Aphrodite, while I am intoxicated with Chimaros wine and throw
> the kottabos for Agathon."

Antiphanes explained how this game was played in his *Hidden from Aphrodite* (Athenaeus 15.666f–667b):

> A: This here is the thing I mean. Don't you understand? The lampstand is a
> kottabos. Pay close attention. The prize is eggs and five . . .
> B: But what for? It seems silly. How will you 'shoot kottabos'?
> A: I will show you step by step; whoever when he shoots at the pan causes the
> kottabos to fall—
> B: The pan? What pan? Do you mean that little thing that lies up there on top,
> the tiny platter?
> A: Yes, that's the pan—he becomes the winner.
> B: How is one going to know that?
> A: Why, if he just hits it, [the pan] will fall on the *Manês* [a statuette representing
> a slave] and there will be a very loud clatter.
> B: In the gods' name, tell me, has the kottabos got a *Manês*, attending it like any
> slave? . . . Take a good cup and show me how you do it.
> A: Like a good flute player, you've got to curl your fingers round the handle,
> pour in a little wine—not too much!—and then shoot. . . .
> B: Poseidon, what a high shot you've made!

Later on, symposiasts were permitted a broader range of poetic toasts, chalices offered to the chosen one in a sentimental declaration of love. They were called "drink the crowns" (Pliny *Nat. Hist.* 30.3.12) and consisted of crushing the flowers from one's crown into the wine and offering it to one's love. A toast of this kind was offered to Mark Antony by Cleopatra, but not as an act of loving kindness. The queen was offended that he always had a taster with him, to try his food before he ate it. To demonstrate that if she truly wanted to kill Antony, she would succeed despite his precautions, Cleopatra poisoned her floral crown, and then proposed to Anthony that he "drink the crown." But just as Antony was about to put the cup to his lips, the queen stopped him; she had a condemned prisoner brought out and gave the latter the wine instead. The poor man had barely finished drinking when he fell dead at Antony's feet.

THE END OF THE DINNER

Afternoons could be a heady mix of food, beautiful courtesans, musicians, flutists, and dancers of both sexes. And above all, wine, about which the poets loved to sing. When the poet Archilochus earned his wage as a soldier, he sang, "My bread depends upon my spear, from my spear comes wine, and supported by my spear, I drink...." Our final word on wine comes from Euripides' *Bacchus* (772): "Wine, antidote to all woes, given as a gift to mortals. Without wine, love would not last and all other human joys would die."

At a certain point the symposium would wind down and friends would go their various ways. Usually it was not late when the party broke up, especially in winter. Though one could always light the rooms with torches, candles, and lamps, light was scarce and expensive. The life of the ancient Greeks was regulated by the sun: one rose early and "went to bed with the chickens," as the saying goes.

With dinner at an end, the men returned to their homes and their wives. If they had not been so drunk and wanton as to wander off with a flutist or courtesan, the evening that had passed under the benevolent eye of Dionysus ended happily under that of Aphrodite.

BIBLIOGRAPHY

Allinson = Menander, *The Principal Fragments*, Francis G. Allinson, trans. (Cambridge, MA, 1930).

Athenaeus, *The Deipnosophists*, C. B. Gulick, trans., 7 vols. (Cambridge, MA, 1969–71).

Diehl = *Anthologia Lyrica*, E. Diehl, ed. (Leipzig, 1949–).

FGH = *Die Fragmente der griechischen Historiker*, F. Jacoby, ed. (Leiden, 1923–58).

Kaibel = *Comicorum Graecorum Fragmenta*, G. Kaibel, ed. (Berlin, 1899).

Kock = *Comicorum Atticorum Fragmenta*, T. Kock, ed. (1880–88; repr. Utrecht, 1976).

Kuchenmüller, G., *Philetae coi reliquiae* (1928).

PLG = *Poetae Lyrici Graeci*, T. Bergk, ed., 5th ed. (1900–14).

Plutarch, *The Lives of the Noble Grecians and Romans*, John Dryden, trans. (1864; New York, 1944).

TrGF = *Tragicorum Graecorum Fragmenta*, A. Nauck, ed. (Göttingen, 1971–).

RECIPES

We have now arrived at the recipe section. Here we will seek to flesh out the notes jotted here and there throughout Athenaeus's *The Deipnosophists*, amending them at times to conform to modern tastes. Aiding us in this endeavor is the fact that Greek cuisine from the Classical era was very simple. Numerous recipes, passed from generation to generation, have endured for centuries and come down to us virtually unchanged. Moreover, we must not forget that Roman cuisine of the imperial age was derived for the most part from the Greeks. We can often reconstruct dishes mentioned by various Greek authors based on analogous Roman dishes: they must merely be trimmed of the excesses that Apicius added during the late Roman Empire. In fact, many of the recipes in *De re coquinaria*, Apicius's opus magnum, work on two levels: one starts with the rich, ancient, traditional recipes, which are then finished—almost as a postscript—with one of the outlandish sauces so beloved in the fourth century A.D. Combining a quantity of recipes gleaned from other Greek authors—including some that are quite comprehensive, such as those of Archestratus of Gela—with a series of accurate and reasoned reconstructions of those that are merely hinted at, we end up with a good idea of what was served on ancient Greek tables.

NOTE TO THE READER: Full recipes here are numbered. Many of the food notes are not full recipes, but we have included them to express the range and depth of ancient Greek cooking. The adventurous cook can experiment with these descriptions as he or she sees fit!

Breads and Flour-Based Foods

We start with the principal ingredient of Greek meals, in fact of meals in all the countries of the Mediterranean: bread. Bread could be bought from the baker, or, if a family was rich, made and baked at home. Archestratus recommends that the bread-maker be a Phoenician or Lydian, "who knows how to make daily every kind of bread, no matter what you order" (Athenaeus 3.112c). In his *Gastronomy*, he writes:

> First, then, dear Moschus, I will call to mind the gifts of the fair-haired Demeter, and do thou lay it to heart. The best that one may get, ay, the finest in the world, all cleanly sifted from the rich fruit of barley, grows where the crest of glorious Eresus in Lesbos is washed by the waves. It is whiter than snow from the sky. If it be so that the gods eat barley-meal, Hermes must go and buy it for them there. In seven-gated Thebes, too, there is good barley, in Thasos, also, and in some other towns; but theirs seem like grape-stones compared with the Lesbian. Grasp that with understanding sure. Supply yourself also with the round roll of Thessaly, well twisted in the maker's hand, which Thessalians call *krimnitas*, but the rest of the world calls *chondrinos*. Next, I recommend the scion of Tegea's finest wheat, baked in ashes. Very fine, too, is the wheat loaf made for the market which glorious Athens supplies to mortals; and the loaf which comes white from the oven in Erythrae, where grapes grow richly and abounds in all the luxurious daintiness of the Seasons . . .
> (Athenaeus 3.111−12).

But these were not the only breads of the ancient Greeks. There were well over sixty kinds of bread, from the rough bread called *quadratus* (square) by the Romans, or *kodraton* by the Greeks, a loaf that is divided into eight pieces with four cuts; to the most refined *boletus*, mushroom-shaped rolls sprinkled with poppy seeds. It is not possible to list them all, but we have cited a few. Where possible, we will give the recipes for them, bearing in mind that flour varies greatly from one place to the next. As for the rest, they were the simple breads from time out of mind, with some supplemental ingredients.

ARTOLAGANON (FOCACCIA)

The name means "leaves of bread." To prepare it the Greek way, one starts, as always, with bread dough, but later adding milk, oil, lard, pepper, and wine (Athenaeus 3.113d). To make it nowadays, one could simply ask for bread dough at a bakery or supermarket and then work in the ingredients indicated by Athenaeus, cooking it in a very hot oven. One could also make the bread dough at home, as follows.

> 3½ cups (350 g) flour
> 1 tablespoon salt
> 1 tablespoon yeast dissolved in ¾ cup warm water
> 2 tablespoons olive oil
> 2 tablespoons lard
> ¼ cup (60 ml) white wine
> ¼ cup (60 ml) milk
> pepper to taste

PERSISTENCE OF ARTOLAGANON IN THE MODERN WORLD
Artolaganon is nothing more than bread enriched with oil, lard, and so forth, and is therefore fundamentally the same as pizza bianca (flat white bread, like the thinnest focaccia made in the U.S.). It is probably similar to the bread that is called Roman pizza by the Romans, and pizza-bread in Lazio, an unconscious translation of the Greek term.

Put the flour in a bowl, mix in the salt, and make a well in the middle. Pour the dissolved yeast and the warm water into the hole, then mix gently. Transfer to a floured board and knead (flouring the hands and board frequently) until the dough is compact, elastic, and smooth. Put the dough in an oiled bowl and let rise in a warm place. When it has doubled in volume (about 20–30 min.), knead it, adding oil, lard, wine, milk, and pepper, and mixing it evenly, adding flour as needed. Then set it to rise again (about 20 minutes). Punch it down and spread it evenly in an oiled rectangular pan; let it rise once more (about 20 minutes). When it has risen, cook it in a hot oven (475° F or 250° C) for about 20 minutes, or until done in the middle and golden brown on top.

Recipe 2

KAPYRIA

Athenaeus claims that this is none other than the Roman *tracta* (a type of dough) (3.113d). In Cato's day, it was made by mixing *alica* (large spelt grains) with flour and water. The dough was shaped round and coated with oil, and was then placed in the oven (Cato De agr. 86).

4.5 lbs. (2 kg) wheat flour
2.2 lbs. (1 kg) spelt seeds
Water added to make a dough, about 1 cup (250 ml) water per pound of flour

Soak the spelt seeds in water until they become soft. Drain them and mash them until they make a compact paste. Gradually add the flour until it is absorbed. When the dough is the right consistency—not too sticky or too dry—mark various "tracks" or lines across the dough that you will make into strips, then roll it out and dry over a rack. Next, rub the strips with an oiled cloth and leave them to dry in the air or in a warmed oven.

Once dried, the strips can be used as pasta with a favorite sauce. Or use durum (hard wheat) flour and water, and continue as above, again making pasta; or you can roll them out round and fry them in oil, dusting them with cinnamon once they're cooled, as a dessert; or cook on an iron grill, over an open flame, and serve like tortillas.

PERSISTENCE IN THE MODERN WORLD
These soft bread leaves seem to be similar to the "pages of music" (*carta da musica*) from Sardinian shepherds: very thin—sometimes baked, sometimes fried—confections. They are also similar to the spaghetti that was made at Torre del Greco up until the second half of the last century, which used hard wheat flour. Once the dough was made it was rolled out, cut, and left to dry, two strands together. This spaghetti was U-shaped and long and had to be cut apart before it was tossed into boiling water. It is interesting to note that in some of Apicius's recipes, *tracta* (the dried dough) came to be used like our small pastas, for example in soup or broth.

APANTHRAKIS

This is a light, soft bread, mentioned in Aristophanes' *Ecclesi-azusae*, where he wrote, "The apanthrakis are cooking." Another type is cited by Diocles of Carystus when he writes that they were softer than *laganon*. Probably, says Athenaeus (3.110b), they roasted these breads in the fireplace ashes as was the custom in Athens. In Alexandria, this bread was consecrated to Kronos, and it was left in the temple of that god where anyone might help themselves.

PERSISTENCE IN THE MODERN WORLD

Today the derivative of this ancient Greek bread is not found in Greece, but in Turkey, where it is called pita. These soft flat breads are filled with something spicy and hot and rolled like a cigar.

5 cups (500 g) flour
1 tablespoon salt
1 cup (250 ml) sour milk (see note)
1 tablespoon yeast dissolved in 2 tablespoons
    of warm water
1 tablespoon honey
1 cup (250 ml) warm water
¼ cup (60 ml) olive oil

Mix the flour and salt and place it in a mound on the table (or a cutting board), forming a well in the center. Pour in the oil, sour milk, honey, water, and yeast. Work the dough in the normal manner (bringing the flour into the wet ingredients and slowly mixing it together with your hands, and then kneading it) until it is smooth and elastic. Place it in a warm place protected from drafts for about two hours. Punch down and knead the risen dough again, and cut it into 10 or 12 pieces. Roll each piece out with a rolling pin to make it round and roughly 6–8 inches in diameter. Place them on a well-greased baking sheet in a warm spot to rise again (30–40 minutes). Finally, bake them for 20 minutes in a hot oven, 375° F or 200° C.

Note: To make sour milk, add ½ teaspoon lemon juice or vinegar to regular milk, and stir to blend.

BOLETUS (BOLETINOS)

Boletus breads are oven-baked rolls shaped like mushrooms (Athenaeus 3.113c). These rolls were probably made with dough enriched with oil and lard. Before leaving the dough to rise, the bread was oiled and strewn with poppy seeds. The seeds would sink into the dough as it rose. Wheat flour was sprinkled on a ceramic baking pan before the dough was placed on it, allowing the bread to take on a magnificent color that Athenaeus compared to smoked cheese.

BRAZIER BREAD

The comedian Antidotus wrote in his play *The Premier Danseur*, "He took some hot brazier-bread—why not?—and folding it over he dipped it into sweet wine" (Athenaeus 3.109c). Crobylus in *The Suicide* wrote, "Taking a dough pan full of brazier bread" (ibid.). And finally, Lynceus of Samos, in his letters to Diagoras, compares Athenian food to that of Rhodes:

> Besides, the bread sold in their market is famous, and they bring it in at the beginning and the middle of a banquet without stint. And when they are tired and sated with eating, they then introduce a most delightful allurement in what is called smeared brazier-bread. It is a soft and delectable compound dipped in sweet wine, with such a harmonious effect that a marvelous result come to one whether he will or no; for just as the drunken man often becomes sober again, so the eater of it grows hungry again with its delicious flavor (Athenaeus 3.109d–e).

This seems to have been a soft focaccia that was cooked in the fireplace or on a grill. Probably this bread was not eaten often, since it was torn in two parts and soaked in wine, likely making it very spongy.

CUBO OR DICE (PAN BREAD)

This bread was square in the form and flavored with anise, cheese, and oil. It was likely harder than modern bread and more like oyster bread (crackers) found today in France and England. Heracleides speaks of it in his *Art of Cookery* (Athenaeus 3.114a)

STREPTIKOS (SPIRAL OR TWIST BREAD)

This bread was made by adding a little milk, pepper, oil, and lard to the dough (Athenaeus 3.113d). It would be like our olive-oil rolls, but with pepper.

Sauces and Condiments for Bread

Recipe 4

MINT SAUCE

"Or even the downy leaves of tender flea-bane [mint]—often again, chopping up fresh pepper or Median cress" (Athenaeus 2.66d).

> 1 oz. (30 g) mint leaves
> 1 oz. (30 g) green peppercorns (pickled)
> 1 oz. (30 g) safflower (also called false saffron)
> pinch of salt
> 1 tablespoon vinegar
> 3 tablespoons olive oil

Crush the peppercorns, mint, safflower, and salt in a mortar. Add oil and vinegar and stir.

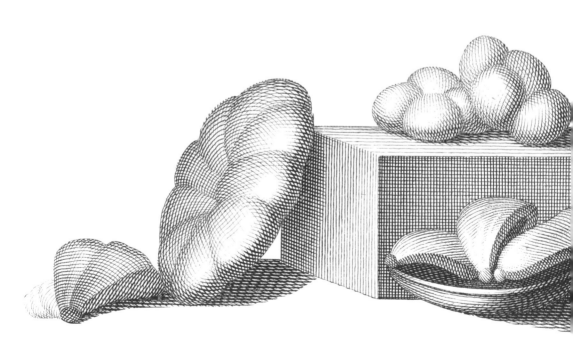

Recipe 5

OXYGARUM

Oxygarum (or oxygaron) was a sauce made with vinegar and garum (the modern equivalent of garum is the Vietnamese *nuoc-nam*, or fish sauce), to which one added other spices and scents in a special receptacle called an "oxybaphon" (Athenaeus 2.67e–f).

Crush together in a mortar:

> ½ oz. (15 g) black peppercorns
> ¾ oz. (45 g) parsley
> ½ oz. (30 g) caraway seeds
> ¼ oz. (10 g) celery seeds
> vinegar
> Vietnamese fish sauce

Mix the paste with 1 tablespoon honey and when you wish to serve it, add 1 tablespoon vinegar and 1 teaspoon of Vietnamese fish sauce. Mix and serve.

Either of these sauces can be rolled into the bread made with Recipe 3 (Apanthrakis).

Appetizers

Archestratus always recommended that appetizers be served with one's aperitif, which in ancient Greece was always a cup of good wine.

> And as you sip your wine let these relishes be brought to you—
> pig's belly and boiled sow's matrix floating in cumin and vinegar
> and silphium; also the tender tribe of birds roasted, such as the
> season affords. But disregard those Syracusans, who drink frog-
> fashion without eating anything; nay, yield not to them, but eat
> the food I tell you. All other common desserts are a sign of dire
> poverty—boiled chick-peas, beans, apples, and dried figs. Yet
> accept a cheese-cake made in Athens; or failing that, if you get
> one from somewhere else, go out and demand some Attic honey,
> since that will make your cheese-cake superb. This is the way a
> freeborn man should live, else down below the earth, even below
> the pit and Tartarus, he should go to his destruction and lie
> buried countless fathoms deep (Athenaeus 3.101c–e).

Regarding hors d'oeuvres, Nicostratus wrote in his *The Pet*, "The first platter, leading the main courses, will contain a sea-urchin, some raw smoked fish, capers, a wine-sop [bread to dip in wine], a slice of meat, and wild bulb in sour sauce" (Kock 2.219; Athenaeus 4.133c).

PEPPER: It was served with the appetizers, evidently to increase one's thirst.

SALTY SNACKS: Salty appetizers were served before dinner, with wine, also to increase the desire to drink.

ONIONS: It seems that onions had the same effect then as now. In fact, Homer wrote, when describing Nestor's dinner, that he gave out onions to chew with the wine (Athenaeus 1.10b; *Iliad* 11.628–30).

CATO'S GREEN OLIVES

The olive was, in antiquity as it is today, the hors d'oeuvre par excellence. Aristophanes, discussing appetizers, pondered pickled olives: "Do you, master, love the ladies who are over-ripe or the virginal ones with bodies firm as olives steeped in brine?" (Athenaeus 4.133a). No exact recipe has come down to us for how olives were prepared in ancient Greece, but in Cato's treatise on agriculture we have various Mediterranean recipes that almost certainly show that olives have always been prepared as they are today.

Cato writes: "Pick the olives before they turn black. Take any growths off of them and place them in a water bath. Change the water frequently and when they are well soaked, separate them and toss them in vinegar, adding oil and 170 grams of salt per eight and one half liters of olives. When you are ready to use them, take them out of the marinade, season them with fennel and a myrtle branch that has been soaked in oil" (*Agr.* 107; 108).

The recipe is clear and needs no explanation.

Note: If you harvest or purchase your own olives, follow Cato's water bath procedure, changing the water daily for a week. The water should have at least ¼ cup of salt per gallon of water (100 g per 8 liters) when soaking the olives. Bags or sacks of olives are also sold in Italy, and in Italian-American markets, in a saltwater brine. Either way, a half-pound of olives, presoaked, or purchased in brine sacks, can then be put in a jar with equal parts of oil and vinegar and let to sit for at least a week, with fennel and myrtle added at the end of the week. Rinse the olives before serving.

OLIVES PICKLED IN FENNEL

"First of all, cover them with cold pickling sauce so that they maintain their color; when there are enough gathered to fill a jar, cover the bottom of the jar with fennel and myrtle branches that have been prepared in a small kettle. Now take the olives out of the pickling, towel them dry, and mix in seeds, completely refilling the jar. Finally, cover the top with dry anise and 2 parts of dry, fresh mustard and 1 of oil/vinegar brine. Olives treated this way will last a year."

Note: See Recipe 6 for the treatment of raw olives. In this case, the oil and vinegar solution should contain fennel and myrtle, with anise and mustard added to the brine. The olives should remain in the brine for several days to a week before they are eaten.

DRIED OLIVES

These are the ripe, bulbous, wrinkled black olives that are found in Sicily. They must have existed even in Archestratus's day, since he writes in his *Hedupatheia*, "Serve those mature wrinkled olives." Clearly these are the same dry olives served today, and as in Archestratus's day they are best when seasoned with fennel. He explains that this is because "in pious memory of Marathon [in Greek, "marathon" means fennel] for all time, they all put *marathon* in the briny olives" (Athenaeus 2.56c).

Recipe 8

SEA URCHINS

The most triumphant of all the appetizers are the fruits of the sea: sea urchins and oysters.

"The best are those full of red or orange eggs. Also quite good are those whose eggs gleam with a gelatinous substance when they are pulled away from the shell. Dress them with honey, mint, and parsley, diced and minced, to bring out the best flavor" (Archippus *Fishes*).

Archippus's sauce for sea urchins:

> **1 tablespoon honey**
> **3 tablespoons vinegar**
> **1 tablespoon mint**
> **1 tablespoon parsley**

Dissolve the honey in the vinegar, then finely mince the parsley and mint and mix the spices into the honey and vinegar. When ready to eat the urchins, split them in two, cleaning away the spine. Find and clean the egg, pour a dollop of the sauce on the egg in the shell, and enjoy.

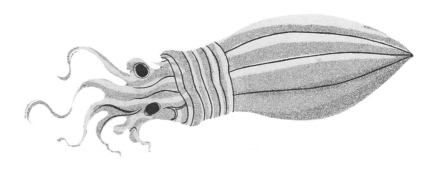

Recipe 9

WILD HYACINTH BULBS (LAMPASCIONI)

Some appetizers were made of ingredients that were reviled by discerning eaters. Athenaeus wrote about a group of authors who evidently did not love hyacinth bulbs and did not share the belief, common at the time, that cabbage or kale protected against drunkenness and hangover. "Goodbye, I say, to sauce dishes filled with bulbs [hyacinth] and kale and to all other cheap relishes" (Athenaeus 2.64a).

Basing this recipe on the ancient one, we see that the basics are always the same. Even if the recipe does not include a method for taking away the terrible bitterness of the bulbs, it is evident that to render them edible, the bulbs should be boiled, with numerous changes of water. Then they are peeled, and a sauce is made to season them.

> **About 10 hyacinth bulbs, boiled and ready**
>
> **Sauce:**
> **1 teaspoon each thyme and oregano**
> **2 cloves of garlic, minced**
> **1 tablespoon each honey, vinegar, and wine must**
> **3 tablespoons olive oil**
> **3 tablespoons minced dates**
> **salt to taste**

Mix all sauce ingredients and pour over the bulbs, adding fresh pepper to taste.

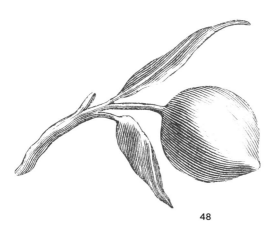

WILD HYACINTH BULBS AS A LOVE POTION

These rose-colored bulbs, which convey a false innocence, are actually a famous aphrodisiac. This seems to have been an accepted fact, going back many centuries, as Martial writes of the bulbs (13.34): "Given that your wife is old and your member is dead, you can only hope to use wild hyacinth bulbs to fill up your stomach." In ancient Greece the hyacinth bulb was widely believed to have aphrodisiac properties; such bulbs could reawaken the ardor of Venus even for the most impotent of men. Here is an old proverb in support of this belief: "Just one hyacinth bulb cannot help you if you are not already a true man." The consumer was thus warned that the hyacinth bulb would do its best in the battle of love, but that it was also necessary for the lover to exert himself. The belief in this aphrodisiac was so strongly ingrained that centuries later, in ancient Rome, wild hyacinth bulbs were served to newlyweds before they went to their nuptial bed. One of these recipes was given by Apicius (7.14.3), derived from Varro. He seems not much concerned with the bitter properties of this plant, recommending simply that one boil them without either honey or cheese as in the Greek recipe. In all likelihood they were none too tasty. Given that the recipe added other aphrodisiacs, such as arugula, it seems he was less concerned with flavor than with their amatory effects. After all, for a successful wedding night, it was the results that mattered: "For those searching for the joys of Venus, boil wild hyacinth bulbs in water, and for the true honeymoon, serve them with pine nuts and a sauce made by boiling arugula and adding pepper."

> 1 dozen wild hyacinth bulbs, already cleaned and
>   boiled several times, or, if already marinated, rinse
>   the bulbs until there is no more oil
> 5 oz. (200 g) arugula
> a handful of pine nuts

Boil the arugula for about three minutes, then drain it and put in a blender with 1 teaspoon pepper. Pour the warm green sauce over warm bulbs and add a sprinkling of pine nuts.

WILD HYACINTH BULBS WITH HONEY

"Look, if you please, at the bulb, and see what lavish expense it requires to have its reputation—cheese, honey, sesame-seed, oil, onion, vinegar, silphium. Taken by itself alone it is poor and bitter" (Athenaeus 2.64e).

Recipe 11

TURNIPS IN MUSTARD

It is not necessary to comment on Athenaeus's recipe (4.133c–d). One can decide what quantities to use, based on the following directions: "the turnip root, you cut in thin slices, gently cleaning away the undried outer skin, and after drying them in the sun a little, either dip a quantity of them in boiling water and soak them in strong brine; or again, put equal parts of white must and vinegar in a jar together, then plunge the slices in it, having dried them off with salt. Often, too, you may pound raisins and biting mustard-seeds with a pestle and add it to them. When cream of tartar forms, and the top grows more and more bitter, then 'tis time to draw off the pickle for those who seek their dinner."

> 4 white turnips, cleaned
> 1 rounded teaspoon mustard seed, crushed
> 1/2 cup (125 ml) oil
> 1/2 cup (125 ml) vinegar

Slice the turnips thinly and put into a pot of boiling water for one minute, and then rinse them and dry them, and let them cool. Stir the other ingredients together in a jar and toss in the dry, cooled turnip slices. Cover the jar, and let the turnips sit for at least two days. They can last about a month and are served directly out of the jar.

Recipe 12

STUFFED LEAVES (THRION)

These are none other than the stuffed grape leaves, called "dolmas," that can be found everywhere in Greece and Turkey, but in ancient times, fresh, tender fig leaves called "thrion" were used instead of grape leaves. In some parts of Greece dolmas are still made with fig leaves, and those who have tried them say that they are identical to those made with grape leaves, though perhaps a bit sweeter. Today, the fillings vary, and this was probably true in ancient times as well. Certainly, rice, the most common filling today, did not then exist, but some other sort of grain filling was used, possibly spelt.

If you wish to follow the ancient recipe, you may use young, fresh fig leaves or grape leaves, but there is also a modern Turkish recipe that suggests using cherry, apricot, or bean leaves. However, grape leaves are currently the easiest to find and use, and one thus may be spared the bother of finding them and boiling them just to the perfect consistency.

This filling can be used with any type of leaf you choose.

> 20 grape or fig leaves, ready (either prepared by boiling fresh leaves, or from a jar already spiced)
> 1¹⁄₈ cup (260 g) spelt or bulgur
> 2 cups (¹⁄₂ liter) broth or water, plus extra for the final cooking
> 1 teaspoon salt
> 3 medium onions, sliced thickly
> 2¹⁄₄ cups (600 g) plain yogurt
> ¹⁄₄ cup (60 ml) olive oil
> 2 tablespoons butter (to soften onions)

If you are using fresh leaves, wash and thoroughly clean them; or use store-bought leaves. Toss them in boiling water, remove them after a few moments, and put them on a work surface. Pick the best ones and set them aside for the dolmas. Select a copper pan that will allow the rolls to snugly fit one next to the other. Use any broken leaves to completely line the bottom of the pan, overlapping to ensure you cover the whole surface; this will help the rolled stuffed leaves stay put during cooking.

Mix the grain and salt and cook until tender in the broth or water. When this is done, pinch off small pieces of the paste, forming them into finger-sized sausage-like rolls of filling.

To stuff the grape leaves, start by stretching out the leaf and placing a roll of filling in the center. Fold up one end and the sides, rolling the leaf around the mixture like a cigar, making them about 2 inches long by 1 inch wide (5 by 2 cm), making sure to tuck in the ends to prevent leakage. If you have enough filling for more than one layer of leaves, make another layer on top until all of the filling is used up. When the rolls are all in the pan, cover the dolmas with broth or water and oil and place a plate on top, to weigh down the rolls during cooking. Cook over a low flame for about one hour, checking frequently to make sure there is sufficient liquid in the pan.

About 15 minutes before the rolls are done, make the sauce: Sauté the onions in the butter until soft but not brown. Add the yoghurt and a bit of the cooking water from the dolmas, and pour this sauce over the rolls just as you are ready to serve them.

GRASSHOPPERS AND CICADAS

There were a few surprising items among Athenaeus's appetizers. We may be grateful that today they have disappeared from the menu, but they were sufficiently appreciated in Aristophanes' day that one of his characters exclaimed, "Good heavens, how I yearn to eat a grasshopper and a cicada (cercopé) caught on a thin reed" (Athenaeus 4.133b; Aristophanes Anagyrus in Kock 1.404).

I don't know whether these insects would have been cooked as Istanbul clams are cooked today, skewered three by three on sticks, floured and then fried, but even prepared this way, I would not be tempted to try them. However, if anyone should wish to do so, feel free. In Africa, they are often talked about and my African nanny assured me that "grasshoppers are sweet as café latte."

Soups and Vegetables

Recipe 13

TISANA (BARLEY SOUP)

Aristophanes mentions *tisane,* a well-known barley soup that was highlighted in one recipe sited by Cato and four other versions found in *De re coquinaria.* All the recipes based on barley were the same except for Apicius's, where he used various sauces.

"Take previously cleaned barley that was soaked in water the day before cooking. Wash and crush the barley. Put it on to cook with water over a high flame. When it starts to boil, add plenty of oil, a small fresh branch of anise, diced dried onion, savory, and a bit of ham and have it cook together until it becomes creamy. Add coriander and salt and serve it up" (Apicius 5.5.1).

> 10 oz. (250 g) white barley
> water (about 4 cups)
> 2 tablespoons olive oil
> 1 teaspoon anise
> 1 minced onion
> 1 pinch of savory
> 1 pinch of chopped fresh coriander (cilantro)
> 1 thick slice of prosciutto or ham
> salt and pepper to taste

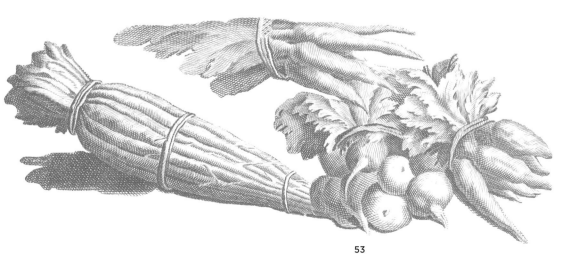

POLENTA (CONDROS)

"But when making a dish of goat, lamb, or a chicken freshly killed, throw fresh grain (barley) in a pan and crush it well, mixing in fragrant oil. When the broth is boiling vigorously, put in the rest, then cover the pan with a lid and leave it to cook, covered, because that way the heavy mixture swells. Serve with a (tablespoon) of new wine" (Nicander of Colophon, fr. 68 Schneider).

> 1 cup (250 ml) cooked barley
> 2 cups (500 ml) shredded lamb or chicken, cooked
> 1 onion
> 1 tablespoon parsley
> 3 sage leaves
> 2 cups (500 ml) broth
> ¼ cup (60 ml) olive oil
> salt and pepper to taste

To make this polenta, one can follow Athenaeus's instructions for barley soup or tisana, Recipe 13, replacing those spices and the ham with the above spices and meat.

The only problem with this recipe is that to make it properly, one should live in the countryside where it is possible to get fresh stalks of barley, which are not found in city markets. You can, however, substitute white barley, or better yet, bulgur from Turkey. Both of these require pre-soaking and then cooking for some hours. It is simpler, of course, to get packaged barley. Both bulgur and this boxed barley are ready for cooking and only require a good crushing in a mortar or a blender, leaving it somewhat grainy, not too fine.

Recipe 15

ZENO'S LENTIL SOUP

Aristophanes always served up modest lentil soup, whether in his *Gerytades* or in his *Amphiaraus* (both now lost), showing that it must be a pleasing potage. He calls it, "the sweetest of delicacies" (Athenaeus 4.158c).

> 1 lb. (450 g) lentils
> 8 cups (2 liters) broth
> 1 large minced leek
> 1 carrot, 1 stalk of celery, and 1 small onion, all sliced
> 2 tablespoons vinegar
> 1 teaspoon honey
> olive oil
> 12 coriander seeds
> salt and pepper to taste

Rinse the lentils thoroughly, then put them into a pot with the broth to boil. Reduce heat and simmer for one hour. When the hour is up, skim the top, add the vegetables and leave simmer again until it is cooked (about 30 minutes). If the soup seems too watery, mix in some cornstarch, or, better yet, pass some of the lentils through a sieve. Now add the vinegar and honey. Pour into serving bowls and add a good dollop of olive oil (about 2 tablespoons per serving), sprinkling on coriander seeds, and salt and pepper to taste.

It seems as if Zeno was pulling our leg with this recipe, as he writes that to finish off the soup, one should add 12 coriander seeds. This commendable precision regarding a quantity is not common in ancient recipes, at least in those that are not medicinal, but assuredly these 12 coriander seeds radically change the flavor of the soup.

CHRYSIPPUS'S LENTIL SOUP

This soup is basically like the one above, but Chrysippus, who evidently loved bitter flavors, recommends serving a soup combining lentils and wild hyacinth bulbs. It is doubtful that this would be a very popular recipe, but, then, there are so many varying tastes in the world. Apicius did not mention such a soup, nor is there an equivalent today, but if you wish, you could make the soup according to Zeno, but adding half a pound of prepared hyacinth bulbs (see method above, at Recipe 9).

Recipe 17

WILD GREENS

Greens and herbs used in ancient times included wild lettuce (dark is best), watercress, coriander, mustard, melon, poppy, onion (as well as the variations such as scallions and leeks), garlic, and celery.

> 2 lbs. (1 kg) mixed greens, whatever is in season
> (I chose chicory, parsley, celery, chard, onions,
> scallions, leeks, garlic)
> water
> 1 teaspoon salt
> 3 tablespoons olive oil
> 1 tablespoons vinegar

Place the cleaned greens in cold, salted water and bring to a boil, making sure not to overcook them. Lift them carefully out of the pot with a slotted spoon or large fork. Season them with oil and vinegar.

In Rome, one can now find a mixture of herbs such as those cited in the Greek recipe. This combination is generally large-leaf lettuce, chicory, arugula, wild fennel, garlic, watercress, and mint leaves. I have never found coriander, melon, or wild mustard in the mix, and onion and celery are sold separately. Certainly, anyone who wishes could add to the list, and cultivated plants are just as acceptable as wild.

PERSISTENCE IN THE MODERN WORLD

Today dishes based on field and wild herbs have changed somewhat, owing to the introduction of New World plants, but they are directly derived from the traditional recipes. For example, the following recipe for "Cooked Water" combines Old and New World foods.

"COOKED WATER"

This is a country soup, which can be served dry or soupy, according to the amount of water used for cooking. Below is an indicative list of herbs, but one could use almost any greens that suit your fancy.

> 1–3 cups (¼ to ½ liter) cold water per person
> 2 sliced potatoes per person
> 1 Jerusalem artichoke (or cardoon)
> hops
> 1 bunch of chicory
> I bunch of salad greens
> I bunch of red poppy flowers
> 1 bunch of borage
> 2 tablespoons of lard
> chopped green pepper to taste
> 3 or 4 cloves of garlic
> 1 onion
> a dash of sage
> basil to taste

The only problem is finding an obliging meadow that will yield all of these soup ingredients. A city dweller could make his/her own list and hopefully get from the greengrocer those ingredients not found in the wild—but be prepared for some strange looks. Be that as it may, if you succeed in procuring all these items, including cardoons (a thistle-like vegetable virtually unknown in the United States), here's how to make the soup.

Put cold, lightly salted water in a pot and then add in the potatoes. When the potatoes are nearly cooked, add the greens, cut into large pieces. Peel the Jerusalem artichoke and chop coarsely. The other greens should be washed and cleaned, discarding any tough or discolored leaves. Next add the lard, pepper, garlic, onion, sage, and basil and stir. Let it boil for 25 minutes. Serve it in a bowl on top of a slice of crusty country bread.

SALAD DRESSING

In *The Woman Who Left Her Husband*, the author, either Diphilus or Sosippus, writes the following:

> **A:** Have you got sharp vinegar in the house?
> **B:** I fancy so, slave, and we have bought rennet. All this I will squeeze together in a nice dish for them, and the salad with sour dressing shall be served for all" (Athenaeus 4.133f).

> **1 cup (250 ml) curdled milk, buttermilk, or sour cream**
> **1 tablespoon vinegar**
> **salt and pepper to taste**

Mix all ingredients, chill in the refrigerator, and pour lightly over salad.

The only problem with making this simple dressing, which is low in calories, is finding curdled milk. You can make your own by adding a squeeze of lemon to fresh milk, or you can use buttermilk or sour cream. The recipe makes enough dressing for four large plates of salads.

Meat

Recipe 19

ALEXANDRIAN MIXED BOILED MEATS

"Following these viands platters were passed round containing many kinds of *meat prepared with water*—feet, heads, ears, jaw-bones, besides guts, tripe, and tongues, in accordance with the custom in shops at Alexandria called 'boiled-meat shops'" (Athenaeus 3.94c).

Alexandrian boiled meats were a mix of various pork bits: feet, heads, cheeks, ears, tripe, intestines, and tongue. In Turkey, another country that grew and prospered under Hellenism, there are still restaurants where the sole item on the menu is *ishkembe shorbasi*, a tripe soup that seems to bear a close resemblance to Alexandrian boiled meats. It is unimportant whether there is in fact a direct relation between the two. What matters is the fact that, in Alexandria, there were special restaurants that served only one particular dish. Twenty years ago in Turkey, each small restaurant (osteria) was tied to a specialty dish. If one did not wish to patronize an Occidental style restaurant, one had to move from restaurant to restaurant in order to get a complete meal. If one had strong legs, a good appetite, and time to spare, this was a diverting way to spend an afternoon or evening. I do not know if this is still true today, but I sincerely hope that in Istanbul one can still move from a *metze* place to one serving doner kebabs, then move on to a fish restaurant for fried clams in pastry, then on to a *chippura*, and finally end the evening with some *loukum* from a great bakery.

> 2 pig's feet
> ½ pig's head
> 2 pig ears
> a bit of pork or beef tripe, according to taste
> heart, lungs, liver to taste
> pig's tongue
>
> 1 medium onion, minced

1 clove garlic, finely chopped

1 small carrot, sliced

½ cup (125 ml) chopped parsley

1 teaspoon pepper

½ cup (125 ml) white wine vinegar (if intestines are
  added, double the amount of vinegar)

Fill a large pot with water and 1 teaspoon of salt for each two quarts of water, and add standard soup seasonings: onion, celery, garlic, carrots, parsley, pepper, and white wine vinegar. Bring the water to a boil, then add the meats, and reduce the flame to medium. Cook until tender (about 30–40 minutes). Serve boiling hot and offer a sauce with it, such as the mint sauce in Recipe 20.

Note: Boiled pig can be very gamey. Using already-cooked head, cheeks, tongue, feet, etc. from the roasted, stuffed pig in Recipe 22 yields a much better result: less fatty and more flavorful. This is especially true of the head and feet, since they are largely fat. The cheeks and the portion between the ears and tongue have the most meat. Our test cook declined to use intestines.

MINT SAUCE

This recipe for mint sauce is similar to the one at Recipe 4, but we found this version less cloying, and more delicious.

> 4 tablespoons dried mint (or 1 handful of fresh mint)
> 1 teaspoon pickled green peppercorns
> 2 teaspoons safflower
> 6 tablespoons (90 ml) olive oil
> 2 tablespoons vinegar

Mint is easy to find and can even be grown in a window box. In bazaars in both Turkey and Egypt, the red pistils of safflower, or "false saffron," are passed off on the unsuspecting tourist, who believes he or she is getting genuine saffron. It is nevertheless delicious. Chop all the spices, or crush them in a mortar. Whisk the mixture into the oil and vinegar, and add salt to taste. Let it sit for at least an hour to allow all the herbs to mingle with the vinaigrette. Excellent with the goat and pork recipes following.

Recipe 21

ROAST KID GOAT

This recipe is from Apicius, but is evidently universal.

"Take the baby goat and rub it well with oil, then toss on pepper, a lot of salt and coriander seeds. Put it in the oven, roast it and serve it" (Apicius 8.6.8).

> ½ baby goat, about 5-7 pounds (2-3 kg), skinned
>   and cleaned
> olive oil
> plenty of black pepper
> 4-5 teaspoons salt
> a generous handful of coriander seeds

Place the goat in a large casserole, coating well with olive oil, and rubbing in the salt and pepper. Before putting it in the oven, sprinkle it with coriander seeds. Place in a 325° F (160° C) oven and bake, basting it with its own juices until it falls off the bone (45 minutes to one hour). Delicious with mint sauce, Recipe 20.

STUFFED SUCKLING PIG

Garden-style suckling pig, according to Apicius: "De-bone the pig starting at the throat, rendering it something similar to a wine skin, and fill it with chicken meatballs, wild doves, and thrushes, its own meat added into meatballs, pitted figs, dried and prepared wild hyacinth bulbs, shelled snails, beet greens, leeks, celery, boiled kale tops, coriander, peppercorns, pine nuts. On top of this, add 15 hard-boiled and diced eggs, and a sauce made from *liquamen* (either garum or dressing from olive oil, vinegar, and spices), mixed with lots of crushed pepper. Brown the pig in a pan and then put it in the oven." Apicius then concluded by suggesting sauces to serve with it.

18–20 pound (4 kg) suckling pig

For the stuffing:
2 thrushes (pigeons can be substituted and are easier
    to find), de-boned and cut into small pieces
1 small duck, de-boned and cut into small pieces
4–6 figs, diced
1 cup (250 ml) cooked kale
1 cup (250 ml) already cooked, dried, and diced
    hyacinth bulbs (see preparation method at
    Recipe 9)
1/2 teaspoon coriander
1 cup (250 ml) chopped leeks
1 stalk celery, chopped
2 tablespoons pine nuts
1 pound (500 g) wheat polenta or fine bulgur, cooked,
    cooled, and cubed
12 eggs, hard-boiled, cooled, and diced (I used 12 —
    larger here than in ancient Greece)
1/2 cup (125 ml) dressing (oil, vinegar, and garlic)

Garnish:
12 oysters out of the shell
12 clams out of the shell

Follow Apicius's instructions above, having a butcher de-bone the pig for you, or doing it yourself if you are brave. Preheat the oven to 450° F (230° C). Lightly mix the stuffing ingredients, adding the eggs and dressing last. Stuff the pig and sew it closed. Rub olive oil and salt into the skin. Cook for 20 minutes in the hot oven to seal in the juices and to brown it. Then turn oven to 325° F (160° C) for about an hour and a half, or until juice comes out clear when pig is pricked with a fork in the thickest part of the thigh.

ROSE AND BRAIN PUDDING

"...I call this rose dish *rodonia* and I prepare it in such a manner that when you eat it, you not only have a designated crown on your head, but are also perfumed within, treating your body to a truly complete meal. Crush the most aromatic roses in the mortar, and then carefully place chicken and pig brains, de-nerved and well-dressed, with egg yolk, then season with olive oil, garum, pepper, and wine. Mix together well and put it in a new pot to cook over a low, constant flame. When the cook opens the pot, everyone present will smell the delicious aroma of roses."

We include this recipe for completeness rather than practicality, because the ingredients are almost impossible to obtain in this day and age. Perhaps someone, maybe a farmer in the Greek countryside, can make this dish. Make sure you use homegrown roses as the commercially raised ones are heavily sprayed.

> 10 oz. (300 g) pork brains
> 8 oz. (200 g) chicken brains
> 2 tablespoons vinegar
> a few slices of onion and carrot
> 2 tablespoons marsala wine
> pepper
> 30 aromatic roses, petals plucked and crushed
> 2 teaspoons Vietnamese fish sauce (nuoc-nam)
> 2 tablespoons olive oil
> 5 eggs, beaten
> pepper to taste

Immerse the brains in cold water for an hour, then drain. Then place them in cold salted water mixed with vinegar and a few slices of onion and carrot. Bring the water to a boil, and then lower the flame and let the mixture boil for about twenty minutes. As soon as the brains are cooked, put them into cold water again and when they are completely cooled down, skin and de-nerve them. Set them aside to dry, covering them with pepper that has been soaked in Marsala wine. Mix the brains with the eggs, the rose petals, the fish sauce, and a little oil. If you do not have a brazier, which could give uniform heating to the dish, follow the Greek formula and brown the mixture first, and then press it compactly into an oiled mold. Cook it in a double-boiler for an hour, or until the mixture is hardened. To test if it is done, stick a toothpick into the flan; it should come out clean. Unmold it onto a plate, sprinkle with pepper, and serve.

Recipe 24

BOILED PIG'S FEET

From various texts we are given to understand that pig's feet were served. Antiphanes in his *The Woman of Corinth*, writes: "And then a little pig's foot to Aphrodite" (Athenaeus, 3.95e–f). That they were served boiled is explained by Pherecrates in *The Miners*: "trotters well-boiled" (ibid., 3.96a); the same author mentioned them again in his *The Slave-Teacher* (ibid., 3.96b).

> 6 pig's feet (ask the butcher to remove the bristles
> and cut them in quarters)
> 3 quarts (3 liters) water
> 1 large onion
> 2 carrots
> 3 stalks of celery
> 2 tablespoons salt
> ½ cup (125 ml) white vinegar
> vinegar and pepper to taste when serving

Put ¾ cup (200 ml) water in large pan with 2 tablespoons of salt and ½ cup (125 ml) white wine vinegar. Bring to a boil, adding the diced vegetables. When the water returns to a boil, add the pig's feet, well cleaned. Cook until they are well done and falling off the bone, about 15 minutes for small pig's feet or 30 minutes for large ones. When they are cool enough to touch, pull the meat off the bones and heap it onto a plate. Sprinkle with pepper and vinegar to taste. Serve hot with lots of fresh bread.

Note: The leftover broth is good for making lentil soup: just add lentils and cook. The spices and meat flavor make for an interesting and delicious soup.

Recipe 25

SMOKED PIG'S FEET

Pig's feet can also be served smoked, and in this case they are served covered in melted, smoked cheese. This dish was once readily available in Rome: one had only to go to a store specializing in *porchetta dei Castelli*, a pig stuffed and roasted whole, highly salted and spiced, which was served at festivals and food stands all over Italy. But recently it has become harder to find.

> 6 smoked pig's feet
> 3/4 pound (300 g) grated smoked cheese
> 1 tablespoon olive oil

Put the pig's feet in an oiled pan and cover it with cheese. Cook for about 10 minutes in a hot oven (about 425° F or 225° C) to allow the cheese to melt.

TONGUE

Aristophanes mentions tongue in a list of alternatives to anchovies (Athenaeus 3.96c). But there is no information as to how they were prepared. Probably, they were boiled and then flavored with some garum (fish sauce).

ORGAN MEATS

Also mentioned by Aristophanes (Athenaeus, ibid.) is a laundry list of internal organs: liver, wild boar kidneys, ribs, tongue, spleen, and piglet tripe, all slaughtered in autumn, which he recommends be served with hot rolls. Dioxippus in *A Foe to Pimps* mentions "sweetbreads, paunch, and entrails" (ibid., 100e), while Eubulus, in the *Deucalion*, lists chicken livers, guts, lungs, and tripe.

SOW'S BELLY

This dish is mentioned by Alexis in *The Man from Pontus*, making fun of the orator Callimedon, who was nicknamed "the Lobster" (or Crayfish) because of his greediness: "Every man is willing to die for his country, but Callimedon the Crayfish would doubtless submit to death for a boiled sow's paunch" (Athenaeus 3.100c).

Boiled sow's belly was served with a sauce based on vinegar and silphium. Keep in mind that silphium (no longer found) had a flavor like garlic. So in our time, obtaining a sow's belly and wishing to eat it—two things that seem improbable to me—it would do to mix vinegar, mixed with crushed garlic and perhaps a bit of oil, salt, and pepper (ibid., 3.100f). In *Man of Science*, Sopater writes: "a slice of sow's matrix not over-cooked, with pungent brine-and-vinegar sauce inside" (ibid., 3.101a).

VULVA EIECTITIA

This was the vulva of a sow that had miscarried. It was considered especially tasty and it was mentioned by Hipparchus, the author of the *Egyptian Iliad* (Athenaeus 3.101a).

The entrails of lamb, goats, pigs, and other domesticated animals were all eaten in antiquity, and many are still served today. However, although they were considered delicious delicacies in former times, sow's vulva and breasts are not eaten today. For these foods, we have Apicius's recipes and we know that normally vulva was eaten boiled and accompanied by a sauce similar to the one listed in Recipe 24 for boiled pig's feet, whereas sow's breasts, once boiled, were sprinkled with salt, put on a skewer, and roasted or grilled or stuffed with "all of god's best." Even if we wanted to try these dishes today, which I doubt, it would be impossible given the mechanized meat-processing systems: after the animal is completely emptied and the parts are butchered, it would not be possible to locate the vulva or breasts of a sow.

Seafood

According to Daphnus of Ephesus, Archestratus took a trip "around the world" to gratify his palate as well as his more basic appetites. (We must bear in mind that his "world" was limited to Greece, Magna Graecia, the Bosporus, and part of the coast of Asia Minor.) Upon his return, he counsels a friend as to where to eat and what to order:

> Eat, dear Moschus, a slice of Sicilian tunny, cut at the time when it should be salted in jars. But the shabar, a relish from Pontus, I would consign to the lowest regions, as well as all who praise it. For few there be among mortals who know that it is a poor and insipid morsel. Take, however, a mackerel three days out of the water, before it enters the pickle and while it is still new in the jar and only half-cured. And if thou go to the sacred city of glorious Byzantium, eat again, I pray you, a slice of *horaion*; for it is good and luscious. (Athenaeus 3.116f–117a)

Then he goes on to list all the known mollusks, explaining where to find the best ones:

> Aenus produces large mussels, Abydus oysters, Parium crabs; Mitylene scallops. Ambracia, too, supplies very many, and along with them monstrous.... and in Messene's narrow frith thou shalt get giant whelk, in Ephesus also the smooth cockles, not to be despised. Calchedon gives oysters but as for periwinkles ("heralds") may Zeus confound them, whether they come from the sea or the assembly, excepting one man only. That man is my comrade, his home is on Lesbos of the luscious grapes, and his name is Agathon (Archestratus, quoted in Athenaeus 3.92d–e.)

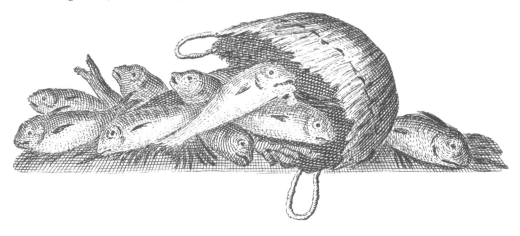

LOBSTER

"Buy yourself a lobster, the kind which has long claws, and heavy withal, with feet that are small, and but slowly crawls he upon the land. Most of them, and the best of all in quality, are in the Lipari Islands; yet the Hellespont also gathers many" (Archestratus, quoted in Athenaeus 3.104f–105a).

> 4 live lobsters, about 1 pound (400 g) each
> 3 tablespoons olive oil
> 1 tablespoon vinegar
> a large pinch of oregano
> 3 tablespoons salt
> pepper to taste

Make a marinade from the oil, vinegar, oregano, and salt and pepper, and put it aside. Slice the live lobsters in half and put them to cook on a grill. As they cook baste them continually with the marinade. Check often to see if they are cooked (in about 5–7 minutes they should turn red in the shell); too much cooking makes them tough and inedible.

Recipe 27

FRIED SHRIMP

"…If you ever manage to get to Iasus, a city of the Carians, you will get a good-sized shrimp. But it is rare in the market, whereas in Macedonia and Ambracia there are plenty" (Athenaeus 3.105e).

> 2 lbs. (1 kg) shrimp
> lots of olive oil for frying
> salt to taste

Put about ½ cup (125 ml) of oil in a frying pan and when it is very hot but not smoking, toss in the shrimp. Fry them for 6–7 minutes, stirring frequently and gently.

AMIA (BLUEFIN TUNA)

As for the amia, prepare that in the autumn, what time the Pleiad is setting, and in any way thou likest. Why need I recite it for thee word for word? For thou canst not possibly spoil it even if thou so desire. Still, if thou insist, dear Moschus, on being instructed here also is the best way to dress that fish, wrap it in fig-leaves with a very little marjoram. No cheese, no nonsense! Just place it tenderly in fig-leaves and tie them on top with a string; then push it under hot ashes, bethinking thee wisely of the time when it is done, and burn it up not. Let it come to thee from lovely Byzantium if thou desire the best, yet wilt get what is good even if it be caught somewhere near this place here. But it is poorer the farther thou goest from the Hellespontine Sea, and if thou journey over the glorious courses of the briny Aegean main, it is no longer the same, but utterly belies my earlier praise (Archestratus quoted in Athenaeus 7.278a–c).

TUNA COOKED IN ASHES

> 2 pounds (1 kg) tuna, cut into pieces
> enough grape leaves to hold the tuna (about 40)
> 4 teaspoons fine salt
> 2 pinches of marjoram

Make a wood fire and let it burn down to embers. Mix the chunks of fish with the salt and marjoram, then roll them up in the leaves, like burritos, so that the mixture is secure inside. Using all due caution, place the rolls on top of the ashes, letting them cook about 5 minutes to a side, being careful not to burn them.

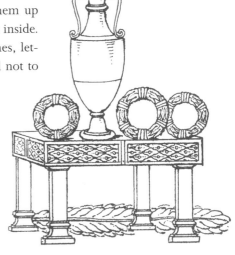

"GONOS"

Ligurian red and Sicilian newborn transparent gobies
Sardine sprats or young sardines
Sea anemones from Sardinia

Count all small fry as abomination, except the Athenian; I mean *gonos*, which the Ionians call "foam" [*sepiolite*, still found today in Sicily, where many old Magna Graecian habits are preserved, particularly the terms for sea life; the little fish called *nunnata* (newborn) are called *grommo*, which means mucousy] and accept it only when it is caught fresh in the sacred arm of Phalerum's beautiful bay. That which is found in ocean-washed Rhodes is good, if it be native. And if you desire to taste it, you should at the same time get at the market some nettles—sea anemones crowned with leafy tentacles. Mixing them with it, bake it in a pan, after you have made a sauce of the fragrant tops of choice greens mixed in oil. (Archestratus, quoted in Athenaeus 7.285b–c)

Evidently, the best way to taste these tiny little fish (*gonos*) was to cook them in an herb sauce.

Archestratus also recommended sea anemones. Given that today these animals are not sold in fish markets, one would have to find them oneself at the seashore. But remember to wear gloves and be careful to keep them far from the eyes. Once harvested and washed carefully under running water, insert a finger into the opening where the anemone was attached to the rock to remove any bits of stone that might remain in its body cavity. After that, clean the anemones again in running water to rid them of any traces of sand and let them marinate an hour in vinegar. A disciple of Archestratus added that, given the small amount of heat needed to cook these little fish and anemones, it was enough just to toss them into a pan that had begun to sizzle.

BITS AND PIECES: SMALL FISH FRY

> 2 lbs. (1 kg) fish eggs, baby sardines, and smelt
>   (in lieu of transparent gobies, sardine eggs,
>   and anemones)
> salt to taste
> oil for frying
> a pinch of thyme
> a pinch of rosemary
> a pinch of oregano
> 1/2 onion, minced

Chop the fish into small bites after cleaning thoroughly and rinsing in salt water. Heat the oil, add the spices and onion, and when the onions are browned, add the fish. At the first sign of sizzling, take them out, and serve them immediately.

THORNBACK RAY

"Eat a boiled ray in the season of mid-winter, with cheese and silphium on it. And so, whatever offspring of the ocean have a flesh that is not too fat should be dressed in this way" (Athenaeus 7.286d). And also, "Scylla's strait in wooded Italy contains the glorious latus, a wonderful food" (Athenaeus 7.311f).

> 3 lbs. (2 kg) thornback ray or skate
> 1 gallon (5 liters) of water
> 1 cup (250 ml) vinegar
> 3 tablespoons coarse salt
> 1 onion
> 2 carrots
> 2 stalks of celery
> 2 bay leaves
> 1 stalk of parsley
> 1 tablespoon pepper
> grated pecorino cheese
> 2 garlic cloves, minced

One eats only the wings and liver of the ray. It is good boiled, but only when very fresh.

Put the water, vinegar, salt, and all the spices, except the pepper, which is added in the last ten minutes, into a pan large enough to hold the ray. Put in the ray and cook over a low flame, slowly bringing the pan to a boil and then lowering the flame a bit more, controlling the cooking. After 10 minutes, add the pepper. The ray should be done 15–20 minutes after the sauce boils: the meat will be coming away from the cartilage. Put it on a plate, and remove the skin (if necessary). Mix the cheese with the minced garlic and sprinkle over the ray. Let the dish sit for a few minutes, so the flavors have a chance to blend.

STEWED CONGER EEL

"In Sicyon, dear friend, you have the head of a conger eel, fat, vigorous, and large; also all the belly parts...," and later, "you can catch a nice conger-eel, which is as much superior to all other fishes as the fattest tunny [tuna] is superior to the poorest crow-fish" (Athenaeus 7.293f–294a).

"I praise all eels, to be sure; but much the best is the eel caught in that part of the sea which is opposite the straits of Rhegium. There, you citizen of Messina, have the advantage over all other mortals, for you can put such food as that to your lips. And yet the Copaic and Strymonian eels bear a very mighty repute for excellence; for they are large and wonderfully fat. In general, it is my belief that the eel is king of all viands at the feast and guides the way to pleasure, though it is the only fish to which nature has given no scrotum" (Athenaeus 7.298e–f).

Here Athenaeus is evidently talking about adult eels on their annual migration to their spawning grounds in the Sargasso Sea; the rest of the time, adult eels live in rivers, lakes, and ponds.

3 lbs. (2 kg) of eel, heads and belly
1 gallon (5 liters) of water
1 cup (250 ml) vinegar
3–4 tablespoons sea salt
1 onion
1 carrot
2 stalks of celery
2 bay leaves
1 stalk of parsley
30 peppercorns

Sauce:
6 tablespoons olive oil
2 tablespoons vinegar
2 cloves garlic, minced
1 stalk of minced parsley
a large pinch of oregano

One only eats the head and belly of the eel, since the rest is nothing but spines.

Slice and chop the vegetables, and add them to the water. Add salt, peppercorns, and vinegar, and, lastly, the cut-up eel. Bring to boil and cook for about 15 minutes. Serve in bowls with warm crusty bread, and add the basting sauce for taste.

BAKED BLUEFIN TUNA

"And have a tail-cut from the she-tunny—the large she-tunny, I repeat, whose mother-city is Byzantium. Slice it and roast it all rightly, sprinkling just a little salt, and buttering it with oil. Eat the slices hot, dipping them into a *sauce piquante*; they are nice even if you want to eat them plain, like the deathless gods in form and stature" (Archestratus, quoted in Athenaeus 7.303e–f).

The ancient Greeks used vinegar as we would now use lemon juice. When lemons were first imported, Greeks and Romans considered them useful only to protect wool from moths, as a preventative against snakebites, and as the best antidote to any kind of poison. Unfortunately, it never dawned on them that the lemon could have alimentary value.

> 2½ lbs. (1.5 kilos) of tuna
> 3 tablespoons fine salt
> 3 tablespoons olive oil
> vinegar to sprinkle over the top just before eating
> (also superb is a mixture of vinegar, oil, and garlic)

For this recipe there is little to add to what Archestratus stated above. Pour the olive oil and salt over the fish and cook at about 375° F (200° C) for 30–40 minutes, depending on its thickness. It is done when the skin is crisp and the tuna comes away from the bone, juicy but not bloody. It can also be cooked directly on the grill, on foil, for about 5–7 minutes per side.

KITAROS (BRILL, TURBOT, OR SOLE)

"As for the citharus [brill], if it be white and hard and large, I bid you put it in leaves in clean salt water and boil it" (Archestratus, quoted in Athenaeus 7.306b).

If you have a large and white brill, boil it in this manner:

> 4 lbs. (2 kg) of brill, turbot, sole, or flounder
> 2 gallons (5 liters) of water
> 1 cup (250 ml) vinegar
> 2 tablespoons coarse salt
> 1 onion
> 2 carrots
> 2 celery stalks
> 2 bay leaves
> 1 stalk of parsley
> 1/2 tablespoon pepper
> grape leaves

Put the cut-up fish into grape leaves and tie them securely with kitchen string. Next chop the vegetables and put them in a large cooking pot with the cold water, the spices, and the vinegar. Place the wrapped fish in the mixture and slowly bring the water only to a simmer; watch it carefully to see that the water does not boil violently. After 15 minutes, check to see if the fish is cooked, as it will depend on how thick the fish pieces are. When done, take the fish meat out of the leaves, discarding the leaves. Pour the sauce over the fish and serve, sprinkling with vinegar, if more flavor is desired.

For a less labor-intensive version, place the fish directly in the stew pot, without the leaf wrapping.

BAKED TURBOT FOR SIX

"But if it be red in appearance, and not too large, bake it after you have stabbed its body with a straight knife, freshly sharpened. Then smear it with abundance of cheese and oil. For it likes to see people who spend money, and it is prodigal" (Archestratus, quoted in Athenaeus 7.306b).

> 2 small turbot, about 2½ lbs. (1.4 kg) altogether
> 4 teaspoons salt
> 6 oz. (300 g) grated parmesan or sardo cheese
> plenty of olive oil

Gut and clean the fish as necessary. Preheat the oven to 350° F (180° C). Just before you're ready to bake, salt the fish. Using a sharp knife, make a series of cuts on both sides of the spine and fill them with grated cheese and oil. Slather the fish with oil and bake it in a well-greased pan for 30 minutes. Also delicious grilled on the barbecue.

SMOOTH DOGFISH

This recipe works for all types of dogfish, such as marlin or blue shark, or mahi-mahi in the United States.

> In this city of Toronê you should buy the belly-slices of the dog-shark, cut from the hollow parts below. Then sprinkle them with caraway-seed and a little salt, and bake. Put nothing else, my friend, upon it, unless it be yellow oil. But after it is baked, you may then fetch a sauce and all those condiments which go with it. But whatsoever you stew within the ribs of the hollow casserole, mix no water from a sacred spring, nor wine-vinegar, but simply pour over it oil and dry caraway and some fragrant leaves all together. Cook it over the hot embers without letting the flame touch it and stir it diligently lest you unwittingly scorch it. Nay, not many mortals know of this heavenly viand or consent to eat it—all those mortals, that is, who possess the puny soul of the booby-bird, and are smitten with palsy because, as they say, the creature is a man-eater. But every fish loves human flesh if it can but get it" (Archestratus, quoted in Athenaeus 7.310c–e).

>
> 2–3 lb. (1.5 kg) slice of smooth dogfish or mahi-mahi
> 3 teaspoons salt
> 6 tablespoons olive oil
> plenty of caraway seeds

This fish is cooked on the grill. Bathe the piece or pieces abundantly with oil and sprinkle them with salt and caraway seeds, then place it on the grill. In some dishonest restaurants dogfish is cooked this way and passed off as swordfish, although the particular taste of dogfish cannot be concealed from the cognoscenti.

You can serve it with a sauce rather than the caraway seeds; one of the best is Sicilian pickling, from the native environs of Archestratus himself. This dressing is made by mixing oil, vinegar, oregano, a few cloves of garlic, and a bit of water. Regarding Archestratus's comment about such fish eating men, don't be impressed: although the dogfish is in the shark family, it is a completely innocuous fish and would never dream of biting anyone. Athenaeus adds that this fish is the same one the Romans called tursio.

Recipe 36

MORAY EEL

"Between [Sicily?] and Italy, under the waves of the narrow strait, lives the lamprey [moray eel] called the floater. If it ever be caught, buy it, for it is a wonderful food" (Athenaeus 7.312f).

> 3 lbs. (1.5 kg) moray eel or yellow eel
>
> Sauce:
> 1 handful of lovage
> lots of oregano
> a large pinch of mint
> 1 onion
> 1 glass of dry white wine
>
> enough water to cover the eel
> 2 teaspoons honey
> 2½ teaspoons salt

Crush together the sauce ingredients in a mortar. Clean the eel well and place it in a pan; cover it with the sauce, wetting it as necessary with wine or water. Cover the eel with this mixture, then add enough water to cover the eel. Cook it on a low flame until it is well done. There should be a bit of sauce remaining.

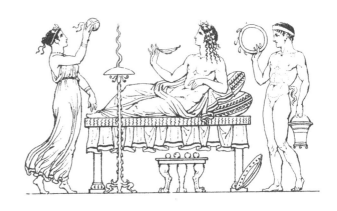

ELECTRIC RAY

"And an electric ray stewed in oil, wine, fragrant herbs with a bit of grated cheese" (Archestratus, quoted in Athenaeus 7.314d).

It will be difficult to taste this dish as one never sees electric eel in the market. However, should you manage to find it, here is the recipe:

> 4 lbs. (2 kg) of electric ray
>
> 4 teaspoons salt
>
> a small glass of dry white wine
>
> a handful of onion, celery, parsley, and carrots to flavor the broth
>
> 3½ oz. (100 g) grated cheese

Cook slowly in a terracotta pot with salt, wine, oil, and herbs, adding the grated cheese at the last minute. Archestratus probably would have used pecorino cheese, not having parmesan available, but it is best with parmesan. You choose. Cover the ray with the cheese and when it has barely melted, take it out of the pan and serve.

Recipe 38

SWORDFISH

"But when thou comest to Byzantium, get a slice of sword-fish, the joint cut right from the tail. This fish is also good in the straight hard by the edge of Pelorum's jutting forehead" (Athenaeus 7.314e).

> 2½ lbs. (2 kg) swordfish
> 3 teaspoons salt
> 3 tablespoons olive oil
> vinegar to taste

This is quite similar to Recipe 32 by Archestratus. Get slices of swordfish about an inch thick, and roast them on the grill, adding a bit of salt and oil per slice. Grill about 2 minutes per side; do not over- or undercook. Serve as is, with a spritz of vinegar (or lemon), or with the following dressing: olive oil, vinegar, salt, oregano, a clove of garlic, mixed with a bit of water; shake it well, or stir with a branch of oregano.

SCORPION FISH

"But in Thasos buy the sculpin [scorpion fish], if it be not bigger than thine arm's length (Athenaeus 7.320.f).

This recipe is from Apicius:

> 2¹/₂ lbs. (1.5 kg) scorpion fish
> 3 teaspoons salt
> plenty of olive oil
> 1 packet (1 oz. or 30 g) saffron
> ¹/₂ teaspoon cumin
> water to cover the fish

Archestratus suggests buying a scorpion fish no longer than your arm (about 20 inches or 55 cm). Clean it well and place it in a pan with all the rest of the ingredients, well ground and dissolved in the oil and a little water. Cover the fish with water, and cook about 15 minutes after the water has come to a boil, or until the flesh comes away from the bone. Take the fish out and continue to cook the liquid until it thickens, adding a bit of starch dissolved in water, if needed. Serve the sauce over the fish.

Recipe 40

PARROT FISH

"At Calchedon by the sea bake the mighty parrot-fish, after wash-
ing it well. But in Byzantium, too, thou wilt find it good, and
as to its size, it bears a back equal to the circling shield. Dress
the whole as I shall describe. After it has been thoroughly covered with cheese and oil, take it and hang it in a hot oven and
bake it to a turn. Sprinkle it with salt mixed with caraway-seed,
and with the yellow oil, pouring its divine fountain from thy
hand (Archestratus, quoted in Athenaeus 7.320a).

> 1 parrot fish, about 4 lbs. (2 kg)
> 6 tablespoons olive oil
> 1/2 cup (300 g) grated pecorino cheese
> 4 teaspoons salt
> 1 teaspoon caraway seeds

Buy a large whole parrot fish. Scale, gut, and wash it. Put it in a
heavy pot, preferably terracotta, and cover with oil, cheese, and
salt. (It is best if you make transverse cuts on both sides of the
fish and insert the salt, cheese, and oil in these cuts.) Put the fish
in the oven at 325° F (160° C) for 30–45 minutes, depending
on the thickness. Once cooked, put it on a serving dish and
sprinkle on a bit more salt and the caraway seeds, adding a good
quantity of oil (if you wish).

BREAM

"Whensoe'er Orion is setting in the heavens, and the mother of the wine-bearing cluster begins to cast away her tresses, then have a baked sarg [bream], overspread with cheese, large, hot, and rent with pungent vinegar. For its flesh is by nature tough. And so be mindful and dress every tough fish in the same way. But the good fish, with naturally tender, fat flesh, sprinkle with a little salt only, and baste with oil. For it contains within itself alone the reward of joy" (Archestratus, quoted in Athenaeus 7.321c).

> 2 bream, each about 2 lbs. (1 kg)
> or
> 1 large bream, about 3 lbs. (1.5 kg)
> 1 teaspoon table salt
> ¼ cup (150 g) grated pecorino cheese
> plenty of olive oil
>
> balsamic vinegar for the table

Make three transverse cuts into each side of the fish, rubbing in a little salt, and putting the cheese in the cuts, and then pour the olive oil over the fish. Roast it in the oven (350° F or 180° C) for 20–30 minutes, or until crispy. Serve it with good quality balsamic vinegar.

Bream meat is quite salty. Other, more tender fish, such as the grey mullet or bass, can be cooked in a similar manner with more salt, and once in a while sprinkled with oil during baking.

Recipe 42

CUTTLEFISH

"Cuttle-fishes in Abdera, and in mid-Maroneia as well"
(Athenaeus 7.324b).

The only recipe found for making cuttlefish in black ink comes
from Apicius (5.3.3). Using what he says as well as indications
from other Greek authors, one can reconstruct this delicacy:
"Take tiny cuttlefish, as they are, with all the blackness and cook
it all together. [Put it in a pan] and add oil, dressing, wine, and
a leek, and green coriander. Cook it thus." The recipe continues
with the sauce suggested by Apicius, that is, the ink, cooked
together with the ingredients listed above by the other authors
(milk, cheese, honey, garlic, and sweet herbs).

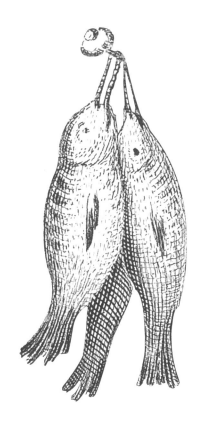

CUTTLEFISH ERASISTRATUS STYLE

Other authors speak about a cuttlefish sauce probably made from its black ink, what they call "blood": Erasistratus writes in his *Art of Cookery*, "It is made with cooked meat, stewed in well-beaten blood, honey, cheese, salt, caraway, silphium (garlic), and vinegar." Glaucus of Rhodes writes in his *Culinary Arts*: "we are dealing here with the blood stewed with garlic and cooked wine, honey, vinegar, milk, cheese, and sweet minced herbs."

> 2 lbs. (1 kg) cuttlefish
> ½ cup (125 ml) olive oil
> 2 cloves garlic, sliced
> 1 teaspoon salt
> a pinch of caraway seeds
> 2 teaspoons honey
> white wine vinegar or lemon juice
> ½ cup (125 ml) white wine
> 1 oz. (50 g) diced feta cheese

Clean the cuttlefish, setting aside the ink sacs and being careful not to pop them. Heat the oil in a frying pan and sauté garlic until it is golden. Remove the garlic, put in the cut-up cuttlefish, and let it fry a bit with the salt, caraway and honey, then add the ink. When it is crisp, add a good sprinkling of vinegar and the wine, followed by the cheese. Continue cooking until the cheese has made a soft sauce.

Recipe 44

RED MULLET

The Greeks held certain bizarre beliefs regarding mullet, a fish they believed was sacred to Artemis the Virgin. If a man were to drink wine in which mullet had been dipped, his sexual desire was roused, whereas when a woman drank the same wine, it would make her calm. This potion, better than today's birth-control pill, would impede pregnancy (Athenaeus 7.325d). Cooked mullet did not have the same powers, but it was reserved for gala afternoon dinners. After praising the mullet from the city of Teichious in the Milesian region, Archestratus continued, "Also in Thasos buy a red mullet, and you will get one that is not bad. In Teos it is inferior, yet even it is good. In Erythrae, too, it is good, when caught by the shore" (Athenaeus 7.325e). Without a doubt, this fish, more than others, owes its quality to where it comes from. In certain locations this fish is full of a disgusting acid.

"Clean it and place it in a pan with a mixture of pepper, lovage, oregano, mint, onion and a solution of one part wine, one of garum or oil and vinegar, and a third part of honey and 'defri-tum.' This sauce should cover the fish and when it is done should be greatly reduced" (Apicius Exc. 16).

> 3 lbs. (1.5 kg) red mullet
> pinch of pepper
> 1 branch of myrtle or a mixture of parsley and celery
> leaves finely chopped
> 1 small celery stalk, minced
> 1 sprig of parsley
> 2 pinches of oregano
> pinch of mint
> 1 onion
> 3 tablespoons Vietnamese fish sauce (*nuoc nam*)
>   or a chopped sardine
> 2 tablespoons honey
> 1 tablespoon brandy
> 6 tablespoons wine
> water

Take a well-cleaned mullet and put it in a pan to fit snugly. Finely dice the onion with all the herbs and the sardine, if used. Mix the honey with the herbs and brandy, and then dissolve it all in wine and a little water; add the fish sauce, if used. Pour the sauce over the fish, and put the pan on the fire. Let it cook at low heat until it is done, about 25 minutes. The bones should be easily removed, and the sauce should have been reduced to become medium-thick. Once all the bones are out of the fish, put it in a bowl, pour the sauce over it, and serve.

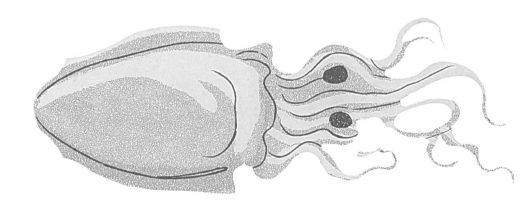

ALBACORE TUNA HEAD

"Buy the head of a large tuna from the deep sea during the summer when Phaeton guides his chariot from the sun in the maximum orbit and serve it boiling hot with a sauce. Also buy a bit of the belly to cook on the spit...."

"Aulopia" is none other than the albacore or longfin tuna. Its meat is the whitest of the tunas and is generally the most delicate flavored. It is certainly the most digestible. Archestratus counsels boiling the head, obviously in water, salt, wine, spices, and vinegar, and then eating it boiling hot. In the West, the head is seldom eaten, whereas in the East, for example, in China and Japan, the head is considered the best part of the fish and is offered to the guest of honor.

One may also grill skewers of tuna steak, marinated lightly in olive oil, vinegar, garlic, parsley, and oregano, with good result.

> 1 albacore tuna head
> 2 quarts (5 liters) of water
> ½ cup (250 ml) vinegar
> 3 tablespoons sea salt
> 1 onion
> 2 carrots
> 2 stalks of celery
> 2 bay leaves
> 1 bunch of parsley
> 30 peppercorns

SCABBARD FISH

In his book *The Art of Cooking*, Mithaecus gives a recipe for cooking scabbard fish of which Epicharmus states: "The beloved ribbon fish [scabbard fish], thin but sweet, and requiring little fire" (Athenaeus 7.325f). Mithaecus prescribes: "Clean the insides of a ribbon-fish after cutting off its head, wash and cut into slices, and pour cheese and oil over them" (ibid.).

The scabbard fish is a silver fish, 2–2½ inches (5–6 cm) wide and a little over a yard (1 m) long. It is not often found in today's market. One good-sized fish should feed about four persons.

> 1 or 2 scabbard fish, depending on size
> ½ cup (100 g) freshly grated pecorino cheese
> olive oil to cover bottom of pan and more for
>   covering the fish
> salt to taste
> vinegar sprinkled on each piece (balsamic is best)

Cut the fish in (2–3 in. or 5–7 cm) portions and oil the bottom of a roasting pan, then arrange the fish in the pan, covering it with cheese and then more oil. If you prefer, use parmesan cheese instead of pecorino, but in Puglia it is still thought best to make this fish with pecorino. Sprinkle a bit of vinegar over the pieces, and then put the fish in a 350° F (180° C) oven for about 15 minutes.

STUFFED SQUID

The comic writer Alexis included the following recipe for stuffed squid in one of his works, as reported by Athenaeus: "As for the squids, I chopped up their fin, mixed in a little lard, sprinkled them with seasoning and stuffed them with finely chopped greens" (Alexi, quoted in Athenaeus 7.326e).

> 4 large squid or 1½ lb. (750 g) small squid
> 1 teaspoon salt
> 2 cups (500 g) diced beet or chicory greens
> 2 cloves garlic, finely minced
> 1 bunch fresh parsley, chopped
> ¼ cup (100 g) diced fat bacon
> pepper to taste
> olive oil

Chop the tentacles with the bacon, adding the garlic, parsley, and greens, flash-fried and diced. Add a pinch of pepper and oil and then stuff the squid with this mixture. Sew it so that the filling does not fall out as it cooks. Put it in a clay pot or shallow roasting pan. Coat the outside with olive oil and a bit of salt and cook at 375° F (190° C) for half an hour.

TRIGGERFISH

"If thou go to Ambracia's happy land and chance to see the boar-fish [triggerfish], buy it and abandon it not, even though it cost its weight in gold, lest haply the dread wrath of the deathless ones shall breathe upon thee. For that fish is the flower of nectar. Yet to eat it or even to catch a glimpse of it with the eyes is not ordained for all mortals, but it is possible only for those who carry in their hands the hollow plaited texture of swamp-grown rope, and are skilled in the practice of tossing pebbles in eager contention, and throwing the bait of sheeps' joints" (Athenaeus 7.305d).

Later on Athenaeus writes: "In Aenus and in Pontus buy the pig-fish, which some mortals call sand-digger. Boil its head without adding any seasoning; simply place beside it a pounded caper-plant, and if thou crave aught else, drop on it pungent vinegar; soak it well in this, then make haste to eat it, even to the point of choking thyself with thy zeal" (Athenaeus 7.326f).

As a child, I caught this fish with simple joy and a bit of bait, but I never wished to grab marsh bulrushes or use stones or sheep's knees. Triggerfish are very tasty and almost all head, but the head has enough meat for a meal.

> 1 large head of a triggerfish
> 1 gallon (5 liters) of water
> ½ cup (250 ml) vinegar
> 2 teaspoon sea salt
> 1 onion
> 2 carrots
> 2 stalks of celery
> 2 bay leaves
> 1 bunch of parsley
> 30 peppercorns

Place the head in cold "court bouillon" and bring it to boil and cook well. Then add the above spices and herbs and fresh-picked capers. (If you do not live where the caper plant grows, you can use capers pickled in vinegar.) Crush them in a mortar or blender, and finish the sauce with the addition of oil, vinegar, salt, and pepper.

Recipe 49

BAKED GILT-HEAD BREAM
"Omit not the fat gilt-head from Ephesus, which people there call ioniscus. Buy it, that nursling of the holy Selinua. Wash it with care, then bake and serve it whole even though it measure ten cubits" (Archestratus, quoted in Athenaeus 7.328a–b).

> 3 lbs. (1.5 kg) bream
> 3 teaspoons fine salt
> plenty of olive oil
> a generous sprinkling of vinegar

Even today Ephesus and its surroundings are famous for its bream, called *chippura* by the Turks. It is cooked for a half hour at 325° F (160° C) rubbed with oil and salt, and served. In antiquity, it was served with a sprinkling of vinegar; today we could use lemon. Either way is simple, and simply delicious!

SALTED STURGEON

"Of Bosporus the whitest that sail forth; but let nothing be added thereto of the tough flesh of that fish which grows in the Maeotic lake [Azov Sea]—the fish which may not be mentioned in verse" (Athenaeus 7.284e). This must be due to the fact that the word for "sturgeon" did not fit Archestratus's rhyme scheme.

We do not know how this dish was prepared. Later on, when Athenaeus discusses sturgeon, there is a critique of Archestratus and his imprecision: "Archestratus, who affected a mode of life like that of Sardanapalus, speaking of the Rhodian dogfish, expresses the belief that it is the same as that which is carried about at Roman banquets to the accompaniment of pipes and wreaths, the slaves who bring it being crowned with wreaths; it is, he thinks, the fish called accipesius [sturgeon]. But the latter is smaller, longer of snout and more triangular than the former, and the cheapest and smallest of them is sold for not less than a thousand drachmas" (Athenaeus 7.294f–295a).

Thus, according to this telling, Archestratus mixed up Rhodian dogfish with sturgeon and declared it to be the fish that the Romans carried to the table, crowned and serenaded with flutes, by slaves in floral crowns. But it seems difficult to attribute this error to Archestratus, who lived in the fourth century B.C., when the Romans never ate fish. The manner of service described in Athenaeus's text appeared in the late second century to the early third century A.D., and more precisely to the Severian epoch, and it was certainly not a ceremony in which an innocuous bottom feeder such as dogfish would have been served.

DOGFISH

"In Rhodes there is the dog-fish, or thresher shark. And even if you must dir for it, if they won't sell it to you, take it by force. The Syracusans call it fat dog. Once you have got it, submit patiently thereafter to whatever doom is decreed for you" (Athenaeus 7.286a).

This fish is the shark most often seen by those who live near the Mediterranean coast. It is not dangerous, given that it feeds on mollusks and small fish. It is eaten fresh, soon after it is caught. Other cookbooks relating to fish do not share Archestratus's enthusiasm. They say this fish is inferior to the smooth dogfish and they recommend particularly spicy recipes to hide its tasteless flavor.

ANGLERFISH

"Where-ever thou seest a fishing-frog [anglerfish], buy it... and dress the belly-piece" (Athenaeus 7.286d). The text says "belly," but I think something there is something off about this quote. In fact, today, we still enjoy the anglerfish, but we eat the tail, which, being rather pulpy, is cut into large slices. Due to its saltiness, it tastes a lot like spiny lobster. I don't believe the underbelly is ever used in cooking.

SOLE

"Then buy a large plaice [sole]" (Athenaeus 7.288a). No guidance here.

"ELOPS" (POSSIBLY MASKED OR FLAG FISH)

"As for the elops, eat that chiefly in glorious Syracuse, since it is the best. For that fish…comes from there, its native place. Wherefore when it is caught off the islands, or the Asian land perchance, or off Crete, it comes to you thin and tough and wave-battered" (Athenaeus 7.300e).

We do not know exactly what this fish is. Greek dictionaries translate the word *elope* as "sturgeon." It is, however, definitively not sturgeon, as that fish is hard to find in Syracuse, nor would it end up skinny and tossed back into the sea at Crete. One can only imagine that this fish may be *Alopia vulpinus*, the thresher shark, which often swims with its fin on the surface of the water and has a tail as long as the rest of its body, giving it the name "flag fish" in Venice.

"LEBIA" (POSSIBLY A TYPE OF SEA BREAM)

It is not easy to deduce what type of fish this was. It was also called *epatos*, which means "liver." Diocles said that it was a rock-fish. According to Aristotle, it was a solitary carnivore with sharp teeth. According to Speusippus, it was a type of porgy. Aristotle's definition coincides with Speusippus' identification, making it probable that it was a porgy. Archestratus recommended buying it in Delos or Tenos.

"IPPURI" OR "HORSE" (ATLANTIC MACKEREL)

One is also not one hundred percent sure if this refers to a type of mackerel, which is even today called "horse mackerel": "the horsetail from Carystus is the best, as in general Carystus is a region very rich in fish" (Athenaeus 7.304d).

GREY MULLET

"Buy a mullet in seagirt Aegina, and you will have the company of charming men" (Athenaeus 7.307d).

COD (OR HAKE)

"As for the cod, which they call *callaria*, Anthedon nurtures it to a goodly size, but it has, after all, a rather spongy meat, and is in general not pleasant, at least to me; yet others praise it very highly; for one man likes this, another that (Athenaeus 7.316a). Archestratus did not give a recipe and it is easy to see why; he did not like hake, and neither do I.

OCTOPUS

"Polyps [octopus] are best in Thasos and in Caria; Corfu, too, nourishes large ones, many in number" (Athenaeus 7.318f).

There is no recipe given for octopus, but they are still served today, not only in Greece but in Italy, where fisherman catch them near the shore and eat them raw after pounding them and rinsing them in the sea, or, as always, boiled freshly caught.

SALPA

"As for the salpa, I shall forever judge it to be a poor fish. It is most palatable when the grain is being harvested. Buy it in Mitylene" (Athenaeus 7.321f).

This fish, called *saupe* in France, is not worthy of a recipe.

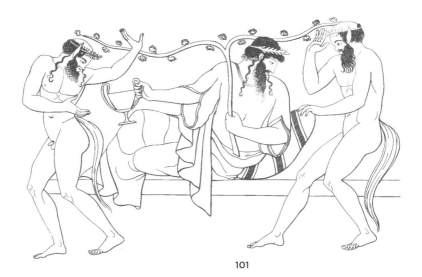

Desserts

Trachemata: in Latin these were called "the second tables." Indeed they were usually carried in on their own tables (Athenaeus 14.639b). These second tables were similar to what we call today our "after-dinner" treats. During the "second seating," salty food as well as sweet was served. The difference was that during the "first seating" a full dinner was served, whereas during the second guests munched on only tidbits, and drank.

There are various lists of what was served for dessert. Philippides in his *Miser* lists: "flat-cakes, dessert (epidorpismata), eggs, sesame seeds" (Kock 3.307; Athenaeus 14.640d). Diphilus in *Telesias* notes "a sweet, some myrtle-berries, a cheese-cake, almonds" (Kock 2.567; Athenaeus 14.640d).

AMILOI (MAHALLEBI)

These are only mentioned by Athenaeus (14.644f). *Amilos* means "starch." Cato writes in the end of his recipe for *amiloi* what to do with the starch: "When the starch is dry, put it in a new pan and cook it with milk." He then makes it clear that one cooked it until it became a cream dessert, although it is not clear whether it was made to be salty or sweet, probably leaving that part up to the cook. On the other hand, for time immemorial, starch has been used to make creams such as *mahallebi* in Turkey or blanc mange in Europe.

> 2½ (625 ml) cups milk
> 2 tablespoons cornstarch
> 3 tablespoons sugar
> 1 teaspoon vanilla (or 1 teaspoon rosewater)

Dissolve the starch in a little cold milk. Meanwhile, put the rest of the milk in a pan over a low flame. When the milk is hot, dissolve the sugar in it and add the starch mixture. Continue cooking, stirring constantly, until it becomes a pudding, about 25 minutes, making sure not to scald the bottom. Stir in the vanilla or rosewater. Usually it is put in a mold, and chilled for at least 30 minutes before serving, although it can be put in a bowl and served warm. In ancient times, rosewater would have been used in place of vanilla, and honey instead of sugar, in which case use only 2 tablespoons of sweetener, as honey is more delicate than sugar.

AMORBITES

What little we know about this dish (Athenaeus 14.646f) is that this is a Sicilian dessert. Given that the etymological root means "shepherd" or "pastoral," it is likely that among the ingredients there were both fresh cheese and honey.

> 2¼ cups (500 g) ricotta cheese
> ¾ cup (175 g) honey

Mix these two together. It is delicious as is, or it can be put in a strudel, between cookies, or even in a cone!

Recipe 52

ATTANITAI

Attanitai is a fried dough dessert mentioned by Hipponex is this verse: "when eating francolin [a game bird] and rabbits, flavor the fried *teganitas* dough with sesame seeds" (PLG 4.2.474). The term for this dessert comes from the word *teganon*, "frying pan." This confirms that we are dealing with fried dough and that this same dough once had sesame seeds added. There is a similar Greek recipe today called *lukumathes*, which can be made by adding grated lemon rind to the batter and using cognac instead of wine.

> 2¼ cups (500 g) plain yogurt or curdled milk
> 2½ cups (250 g) flour
> 4 tablespoons white wine
> pinch of salt
>
> light oil for frying
> ½ cup (125 ml) honey
> cold water
> sesame seeds on a plate (for rolling the dough after
>   the honey has been drizzled over it)

Whisk together the curdled milk, wine, and salt. When well mixed, add the flour to make a paste that is soft and elastic. (If the weather is humid, more flour may be needed.) Let the dough chill for two hours in the refrigerator. Put a light oil in a deep pan for frying, and when it begins to smoke, drop small spoonfuls of dough—3–4 at a time—into the oil and fry them until they swell and are well browned. Take them out and drain them on paper towels. Heat the honey, diluting with a little cold water to make medium thick syrup. Slather the fried dough with enough honey to soak in, and then roll the honeyed ball in sesame seeds.

Makes about two dozen.

BASYNIAS

In the second volume of Semos's *History of Delos* (FHG 4.493), he states: "On the island of Hecate the people of Delos offer to Iris the *basyniai*, as they are called. They consist of dough from wheat flour boiled with honey, to which are added so-called *coccora* [probably pomegranate seeds], a dried fig and three walnuts" (Athenaeus 14.645b). Most likely this treat is the forerunner of Neapolitan *struffoli*, a very sweet and elegant dessert of fried dough, held together with a sugar frosting, which has ancient roots in this part of Magna Graecia. It is therefore possible to reconstruct it with only minor changes. There were no oranges in classical times: this fruit was introduced from China into Europe at a later date. Lemons, on the other hand, were found in much of the classical world. In one of Antiphanes' comedies (367 B.C.) he speaks of lemon seeds, a rarity that was just being gifted to the Athenians from the Great King himself, but they were not yet part of the food system. Athenaeus affirms that in the second century A.D., although the lemon had a delightful fragrance, the fruit was inedible. It was used only in cupboards and drawers to protect wool from moths (Athenaeus 2.83a−f). There was also a belief that boiling a whole lemon in Attic honey until the lemon completely dissolved made syrup that both Greeks and Romans believed to be a protection against every poison, if taken medicinally in the morning.

> 3 cups (300 g) flour
> 8 eggs
> 2 egg yolks
> 2 tablespoons lard or olive oil for frying
> 1 pinch of salt
> 1 cup (250 ml) honey
> pomegranate seeds
> 4-5 dates, cut in pieces
> a dozen walnuts, chopped

Place the flour on a work surface and make a well in the middle. Put the eggs, egg yolk, salt, and 1 tablespoon of lard in the middle and mix together to form a dough. Roll it out rather thick, about ½ inch, and cut into long rows, then cut the rows into pieces about one inch long. Fry the pieces in a deep frying pan with hot oil until uniformly browned. Heat the honey in a double boiler, and, when hot, drop the fried dough in and coat well. Then pile the dough balls on top of each other, making a cone. If any honey remains, pour it over the top, to allow the whole mass to stick together. Finally, decorate with pomegranate seeds, dates, and nuts. Yield: about 30 fried balls of dough.

CATO'S ENCHYTOI

Menander mentions these in *False Heracles* (Kock 3.148; Allinson 458), and Athenaeus includes them in his section on *plakous* (14.644c). The Loeb edition of Athenaeus erroneously translates this dessert as a "molded" cake. The name in fact comes from a Greek verb that means "turned back on itself" or "twisted." Were it not for Cato's recipe, the others would be considered valid. The *enchyti* dough is "twisted," but not in a mold; it is made by squeezing the dough through a tube to fall in spirals into hot cooking lard. It was the oldest known dessert and a representation of pastry chefs cooking it is found in the tomb of Ramses IV in the Valley of the Kings, in Egypt. It seems that this presentation mirrors that described by Cato and therefore was eaten in ancient Greece.

This is Cato's recipe:
"Make 'enchytoi' the same way you make 'balloons,' but use a cloth with a hole in it to press the dough through, in spirals, into boiling fat, about the size of two sticks. When they are ready, cover them with honey and heat them at a moderate temperature. Serve them with honey and a sweet wine" (*De agr.* 80).

> **14 oz. (500 g) ricotta cheese**
> **1½ cups (150 g) flour**
>
> **plenty of olive oil or lard for frying**

Make the dough and place it in a cookie press or pastry bag, and let it fall in spirals into the boiling (smoking) fat, making sure to keep the spiral whole. It should be about 2 inches (6 cm) long. When it is brown, take it out and put it on paper towels to dry. When all the dough it cooked, put the pastries on a plate, cover them with plenty of honey, and allow it soak in. Warm them in a moderate oven (300° F or 150° C) for a few minutes just before serving them.

Recipe 55

PLAKOUS (STRUDEL)

Athenaeus talks at length about this dessert. He cites Demetrius of Scepsis; in his twelfth-century book of *Trojan Battle Order*, there was a city named "Thebes under Plakos" (*Iliad* 6.396 – 97). It seems that the word means "plate," which is to say that the *plakous* was squashed flat. Clearly Cato's *plakous* was not flat, but, although layered; it was probably flat on top. In Greece there were an endless number of *plakous* and Athenaeus discusses which were most delicious. The best were considered those from Paros, so that Alexis in his *Archilochus* has one of his characters exclaim, "O you fortunate old man, dwelling in happy Paros, which country out of all in the world produces the two things most fair, marble to grace the Blessed, and [plakous] for mortals!" (Athenaeus 14.644b–c). Sopater in his farce *The Suitors of Bacchus* (Kaibel 192) extols the quality of Samos's *plakous*, writing, "Samos, whose name is [plakous] maker" (Athenaeus 14.644c).

Cato's recipe:

> Take two pounds of wheat flour to make the outside layer, plus four pounds of flour and two of spelt to make the layers. Soften the spelt in water and when it is swollen, put it in a clean kneading trough after having dried it, then make the dough. When it is well mixed, slowly add the four pounds of flour. Then, roll out the dough and make layers, and put them in a basket to dry. When they are dry, line them up and clean them with a cloth soaked in olive oil, and then cook them. Next, take the two pounds of flour; make bread dough, mixing with water, to make more layers of dough. Take 14 pounds of fresh goat cheese, put it in water and make it soft, changing the water at least three times. Then, squeeze it, put it in a mortar and through a sieve, and then mix it with four pounds of honey. Now, take a clean pan 8 inches by 8 in [30 cm by 30 cm] and cover it with bay leaves basted in oil. On top of this, place the large layer, extending over the sides of the pan, and start to make the *plakous*. Put down a layer of dough, cover it with the cream, then another pastry layer and another of cream, continuing until you finish all

the dough and all the cream, ending with a layer of dough on top. Then make sure all the filling is inside and close it all in with the overhanging outside layer. Cook the *plakous* on a fire with a chimney [a big terracotta vase similar to our country stoves] around which you can place coals, and even cover the chimney with them. Cook long and slowly and check every so often to see if it is done. When it is done, spread lots of honey over it." (Cato *De agr.* 76).

2 cups (500 g) flour
enough water to make dough (see Recipe 2, Kapyria)
light olive oil
pinch of salt

5 layers of dough (made as directed or bought
    ready-made)
1¼ cups (300 g) ricotta
¾ cup (200 g) honey
6–8 bay leaves

Note: You can save a lot of time by purchasing frozen puff pastry sheets, and indeed your results may be rather better. For those who wish to make their own dough, first mix together water and flour, and then divide it into five parts, rolling out the dough very thin, about half as thick as pie dough. Next, let it dry, and once dry, brush with oil and put in the oven to dry again.

Mix the ricotta and honey. Cover the bottom of a baking dish with bay leaves greased with olive oil and place a large layer of dough, covering the pan and overlapping the sides, on top of the leaves. Then take one of the layers of dough, cut to fit the pan, and place it on top of the overlapping layer. Whatever dough you chose, cover it with a layer of ricotta and honey and continue alternating a layer of dough and then a layer of ricotta/honey until the filling and the pastry are all used up. Finally, pull the edges of the bottom layer over the entire dessert, oil it and bake it at 325° F (165° C) for 20–30 minutes, checking for an even brownness. When it is golden brown, take it out of the oven and bath in abundantly in honey.

TAGENITES

"Flooding these fried *attanitai* in honey" ["*attanon*" means frying pan in Ionic dialect] (PLG 4.2.474).

In fact, Athenaeus describes this dessert as a "*plakous*" fried in oil and called "*taynvia*" (Athenaeus 14.646e). They are mentioned by Magnes and also by the writer of the second edition of *Dionysus* (Kock 1.7): "Have you ever watched to see the hot pancakes steaming when you pour honey on them?" And Cratinus, in *The Laws*, says: "And the hot pancakes in the morning throwing out vapour" (Kock 1.52). From these excerpts in Athenaeus's text, we see that *tagenites* were eaten for breakfast. To have an immediate leavening effect, curdled milk was added. In the days before pasteurization, and before milk came in sterile containers, it was easy to come by curdled milk. Today, this type of pancake is made in America with cottage cheese or ricotta.

> 2 cups (500 g) flour
> ¼ cup (60 ml) white wine
> ¼ cup (60 ml) curdled milk (add a teaspoon of
>   lemon juice to regular milk)
> ½ teaspoon salt
>
> olive oil to grease the pan
> honey for the "dressing" on the cooked pancakes
> sesame seeds

Mix first four ingredients until smooth, and cook in small amounts, forming a circle on a greased frying pan, turning over when mixture bubbles, to brown evenly on both sides. Serve hot, with honey and a sprinkle of sesame seeds on top.

AMPHIPHON

Amphiphon means "light all around" and we know that this was a dessert served with candles as an offering to Artemis. Philochorus (FHG 4.493) tells us that the name of *amphiphon* arose from the fact that this dessert was carried to Artemis's temple on the seventeenth day of the month of Munichion (April) because that is the day when the sky is twice as bright as usual. This ritual probably involved various types of desserts, but not one of the recipes for them was given (Athenaeus 14.645a).

CHARISIOS

Aristophanes mentions *charisios* in his *Men of Dinnerville* (Kock 1.442): "For us two I will bake a grace-cake [*charisios*] to eat when evening comes" (Athenaeus 14.646b).

CHORIA

Sweets made with milk and honey (Athenaeus 14.646e). The presence of honey makes it clear that this was a dessert.

DIAKONION

A type of thin bread, like focaccia: it is identified no better than that. Pherecrates refers to it (Kock 1.194). Kock thinks it might be a flat cake made by slaves or *diakones*, or a base for *plakous* that was not very good, so the author did not bother to give any instructions for how to make it. This is based on a quote from Pherecrates: "he began to eat the *diakonion* though he already had an *amphiphon*" (Athenaeus 14.644f).

DESSERT OF ZEUS

This was a dessert made by roasting together grain called *leuke* (probably white barley), chickpeas, cardamom, and small thin breads first soaked in milk and honey, and then served with a saffron sauce (Athenaeus 14.643.b).

ECHINOS

Lynceus of Samos speaks of this dessert in his *Letter to Diagoras* (Athenaeus 14.647a). He states that this delicate pastry was made in Rhodes and that his friend explained how it was made. Unfortunately, the recipe was not given.

ELAPHOS

This was a dessert in the shape of a deer made for the festival of the Elaphebolia (Athenaeus 14.646e). It was made from spelt (today we would substitute durum flour), honey, and sesame seeds.

EMPEPTAS

Seleucus (Athenaeus 14.645d) defines this as a pie made with baked cheeses, more or less similar to the French "vol au vent" but likely much harder and heavier, more like the breadbaskets made into bowls today.

ENKRIDES

This is small, fried dough covered in honey. So says Aeschylus. *Enkrides* are also mentioned by Stesichorus (PLG 3.206; Athenaeus 14.645e); by Epicharmus; in *Hand-to-Mouth Toilers* by Nicophon (Kock 1.779); by Aristophanes in *Danaids* (Kock 1.457); and by Pherecrates in his *Good-for-Nothings* (Kock 1.168).

EPICHYTON

Nicophon mentioned *epichyton* in a list of dessert breads and focaccias in his *Hand-to-Mouth Toilers* (Kock 1.778; Athenaeus 14.645b–c). It appears to be fried dough, which Pamphilus says were also called *attanitai*. (See Recipe 52.)

EPIDAITRON

This was a pastry made from barley flour, served after dinner, as explained by Philemon in his *On Attic Words* (Athenaeus 14.646b).

EPIKYKLIOS

These were Syracusan sweets and from the name as translated it is a type of doughnut. Epicharmus cites them in his *Earth and Sea* (Kaibel 95; Athenaeus 14.645e–f).

GLYKINAS

In Seleucus's *Glossary*, this dessert is said to have been made in Crete, from grape syrup and olive oil (Athenaeus 14.645d). Although flour was not mentioned, it must have been part of the recipe.

GOUROS

Solon says that this is a lentil-based dessert, as referenced in his *Iambic Verses* (PLG 2.58; Diehl 1.38; Athenaeus 14.645f). It is unclear whether this recipe used flour and lentils, or flour made from lentils, similar to bean-flour desserts currently made in Japan.

ITRION

This was a soft cookie made with sesame and honey as mentioned by Anacreon (PLG 260; Athenaeus 14.646d); by Sophocles in *Eris* (TrGF 174) and by Aristophanes in his *The Acharnians* (1092).

KREION

This was a type of flat bread that a newlywed gave to her husband as a gift. It was cooked on a brazier and covered in honey, and it was also served to the friends of the newlyweds. So states Philitas in his *Irregular Words* (Kuchenmüller, frag. 37; Athenaeus 14.645d).

KRIBANAI

These seem to be different than the *kribanites* that are mentioned in the chapter on breads. Sosibius, in the third chapter of *On Alcman*, says that they are shaped like breasts and that the Spartans served them at dinners for women, when the young girls were preparing to sing a hymn of praise in honor of a bride (Athenaeus 14.646a).

KRIMNITES

This alludes to a dessert that was made with unrefined barley flour (called *krimnon* in Greek) (Athenaeus 14.646a).

KROTETA

Probably this was a crunchy dessert, at least according to the Italian editor Rocci. The name supports this guess. The literal translation of the phrase is: "*kroteta*, liberally soaked in thick sauce [honey] from the humming-winged bee" (Athenaeus 14.640b).

MYLLOI

Heracleides of Syracuse recounts in *On Institution* that the last day of the feast of Thesmophoria in Syracuse, a dessert made of sesame and honey was shaped like women's sexual organs; it came to be known as *mylloi* in Sicily. This dessert was paraded around in honor of the goddess (Athenaeus 14.647a).

NANOS

Thin bread made with cheese and olive oil. Given that the text uses the word *artos*, which means bread, it is evidently a flour-based recipe; it is probably the precursor of libum (Athenaeus 14.646c).

NASTOS

We only know that this was a dessert with a delicious filling (Athenaeus 14.646e).

NEELATA

Demosthenes mentions this in his prayer to Ctesiphonus (*De Cor.* 260). Harpocrates says that they are made with dough of roughly crushed barley and honey, which is then cooked and covered in grapes and chickpeas (Athenaeus 14.645b). The dough was stretched thin.

PAISA

Small desserts eaten at Kos (Athenaeus 14.646f).

PSOTHIA

This is a significantly crumbly dessert. In his *Good-for-Nothings*, Pherecrates says, "But in Hades you will receive a good-for-nothing and crumbs [*psothia*]" (Kock 1.168; Athenaeus 14.646c). (In the work of Pherecrates, money in the kingdom of the dead was called a "good for nothing," and was worth two crumbs.)

SESAMIDES

These spherical sweets were made with toasted sesame seeds and honey. In the Pergamon region, these desserts are still made today (Athenaeus 14.646f).

SESAMOTUROPAGA

These sweets were made with sesame seeds and cheese fried in olive oil, covered with celery seeds (probably toasted) (Athenaeus 14.643c). It is believed the name of this dessert was given by Philoxenus of Chythera, who used complex words and phrases made up of other words, much like those in German. He was teased by Antiphanes in his *Third-Rate Actors* (Kock 2.102), who praises him as an inventor of many special words in a jumbled language.

STAITITAI

These were crepes made with spelt seed flour and honey (Athenaeus 14.646b). Epicharmus mentions them in *The Marriage of Hebe* (Kaibel 100). A very liquid dough was thinly spread on the frying pan and when cooked, sprinkled on top with honey, sesame seeds, and fresh cheese, according to Iatrocles' instructions.

STREPTOI

The name leads us to believe that these were doughnuts (Athenaeus 14.645b). Demosthenes mentions them in his prayer in honor of Ctesiphon in the play *On the Crown* (*De Cor.* 260).

SWEETS

Not better identified. One of the Deipnosophists, Ulpian, says that he would definitely eat "sweets" that were creamy or soft, in which case, he would ask for a *mystilen* (a piece of bread dough baked in the shape of a spoon to serve as an edible utensil for eating liquids or semi-liquids. There is an example of a *mystilen* in the Museum of Cairo). The only thing we know about this dessert is that many pine nuts were mixed into it, and the nuts were called by two different names, *ostrakis* and *kokkalos*.

TURAKINAS

Thin bread made with cheese, similar to dough suggested by Cato. These were served with honeyed milk (Athenaeus 14.643c).

Condiments, Flavorings, and Seasonings

Antiphanes lists spices and flavorings that every ancient Greek cook should have on hand: dried grapes (raisins), salt, silphium (a garlic-like bulb), cheese, thyme, sesame seeds, soda, myrrh, cumin, honey, marjoram, dates, vinegar, olives, herbs for spicy sauces, capers, egg, salted fish, watercress, grape leaves, and curdled milk.

CARAWAY SEEDS

This spice is easy to grow and if the seeds are dispersed, the plant will seed itself. Wild caraway has smaller seeds than the cultivated plant and also has a more pronounced flavor.

CORIANDER (Coriandrum sativum)

Both the leaves and seeds of this plant are used, but one should be aware that each has a distinctive flavor. It is not commonly found in Italy, but it is very popular in Asia and the Americas. Fresh coriander or cilantro is sold in bunches, like parsley, and the leaves look similar, but parsley and coriander leaves have very different flavors. It is well to bear in mind that a certain proportion of the population has an almost allergic reaction to cilantro, swearing that it tastes as bad as, or worse than, soap. The name "coriander" comes from the Greek *koris*, which means *cimex*, an insect, presuming a similarity between the odor of the bug and that of the green leaves of the plant. Coriander seeds, however, are milder and seem not to provoke the same reaction as the leaves.

CUMIN

Cumin is a well-known spice to both ancient and modern peoples (Pliny Nat. Hist. 10.161, 20.161).

GARUM

Mentioned frequently in Athenaeus (see 2.67c), it was one of the ancient Greek seasonings that he most disdained. An equivalent sauce is still used with excellent results in the cooking of various Asian countries. This product, called *nuoc-nam*, is sold in many Eastern specialty food stores in Europe and the Americas. If not available, you can make this universal sauce yourself: dry and salt fish, then take the resulting liquid and add olive oil.

LOVAGE

This is called *ligusticum* in almost all the recipes from *De re coquinaria*. It can be found in gardening and plant stores, and can be grown in window boxes or other garden containers. The leaves have an agreeable flavor that falls somewhere between celery and parsley. One could, therefore, substitute for lovage with a mixture of parsley and celery in recipes.

MARJORAM (Athenaeus 2.68a)

MINT (*Mentha pulegium*)

MYRRH (Athenaeus 2.66a)

"OXYMEL" (ibid.)
Evidently a combination of vinegar and honey

"OXYRHODINON" (ibid.)
Probably rose-flavored "oxymel" (vinegar and honey)

SAFFLOWER

This is "false saffron." It is sold throughout the Middle East and in Egypt and is often mistaken for saffron by naive tourists. It has reddish pistils, and when added to a dish, gives the color, although not the flavor, of saffron. It was often used in antiquity as a dyestuff.

SILPHIUM

Silphium is the most famous spice found in antiquity, a wild plant from Syria that grew in the steppes of Africa and that disappeared around the time of Nero. Antiphanes, in his *Unhappy Lovers* (Kock 2.173), teases the Syrians who seem to talk of nothing but cabbages and silphium: "I will not sail back to the place from which we were carried away, for I want to say goodbye to all—horses, silphium, chariots, silphium stalks, steeple-chasers, silphium leaves, fevers, and silphium juice" (Athenaeus 3.100f). This makes the Syrians seem a bit fixated!

THYME (*Thymus vulgaris*)

VINEGAR

We find lists of various kinds of vinegar with descriptions of their benefits and defects. Greek writers called vinegar the "best of the seasonings." The philosopher Chrysippus said that the best vinegars were those from Egypt and Cnidus. On the other hand, Aristophanes preferred vinegar from Sphettus and he also mentioned one from Cleonae, but given that there is a "Cleonae" in Argos, Athos, and Phocis, we do not know to which region he referred. The vinegar from Decelea was also mentioned, but not favorably. In fact, the comedian Alexis (Kock 2.400; Athenaeus 2.67e) wrote, "After compelling me to drain four cups of Decelean home-made vinegar [evidently meaning the awful wine of this region], now you drag me straight through the market."

Index